THE
RELATIONSHIP
ADVANTAGE

Become a Trusted Advisor and
Create Clients for Life

TOM STEVENSON & SAM BARCUS

Dearborn™
Trade Publishing
A **Kaplan Professional** Company

This publication is designed to provide accurate and authoritative information in regard to the subject matter covered. It is sold with the understanding that the publisher is not engaged in rendering legal, accounting, or other professional service. If legal advice or other expert assistance is required, the services of a competent professional person should be sought.

Vice President and Publisher: Cynthia A. Zigmund
Acquisitions Editor: Michael Cunningham
Senior Managing Editor: Jack Kiburz
Interior Design: Lucy Jenkins
Cover Design: Jody Billert, Billert Communications
Typesetting: the dotted i

© 2003 by Tom Stevenson and Sam Barcus

Published by Dearborn Trade Publishing
A Kaplan Professional Company

Printed in the United States of America

03   04   05   10 9 8 7 6 5 4 3 2 1

Library of Congress Cataloging-in-Publication Data

Stevenson, Tom, 1943-
    The relationship advantage : become a trusted advisor and create clients
for life / Tom Stevenson and Sam Barcus.
       p.   cm.
    Includes index.
    ISBN 0-7931-7026-5 (6x9 hardcover)
    1. Customer relations.   I. Barcus, Sam W.   II. Title.
HF5415.5.S738 2003
658.8'12—dc21

2003009490

Advance Praise for *The Relationship Advantage*

"NewLeaf Partners and its relationship management teachings are not new to COMPAREX. For the past two years, we have worked with them, immersing ourselves in their Value Compass methodology, applying it to a variety of customer opportunities with excellent results. For us, *The Relationship Advantage* is a great complement to our efforts toward building and maintaining long-term customer relationships."

—Roland Schweyer, Executive Vice President Sales and Member of the Executive Board, COMPAREX Group

"With all of the interest in reality shows on television today, it is only natural that someone would decide to write a reality book about building and sustaining customer relationships. *The Relationship Advantage* is that book. As vice president at Cisco, I watched firsthand the results Tom and Sam achieved with our Channel Partners through their Value Selling Tour. The principles in this book have been proven hundreds of times in the field with customers and partners. If you follow their advice, I cannot imagine how you could not achieve similar results."

—Clayton A. Reed, Retired Vice President Customer Advocacy, Cisco Systems

"Increasingly, customers are demanding solutions that provide added value, solutions that guarantee a distinctive market presence and a competitive advantage. Finding appropriate answers to these questions requires a competent and reliable partner. *The Relationship Advantage* examines and exposes the culture, behaviors, and techniques that are mandatory for developing effective customer partnerships in a changing European business climate."

—Hans-Peter Quadri, CEO, Swisscom Enterprise Solutions

"Get the relationship right and you win. *The Relationship Advantage* spells it out for you in its most basic terms. Sincere interest in what's important to your customer builds trusted business relationships that stand the test of time. The accounting and consulting professions have been living by these tenets for over 100 years. Every business manager can learn something from this book. Read it, then read it again while you're writing your personal success plan for the year."

—Joseph R. Tort, Partner, PricewaterhouseCoopers LLP

"A basic reason Nestlé has grown to be the world's largest food company is that customers have learned to trust our brands and the people behind them. For Nestlé, continued economic success depends on winning the customer's trust every day in every country where our products are sold. The major theme of *The Relationship Advantage* is that the real sales leadership challenge is winning trust. The book describes how trust is built over a period of time through shared experience, through consistency in word and deed, and from the courage to say things clearly and straightforwardly."

—Stephan Issenmann, Vice President Strategic Marketing and Sales, Nestlé S.A.

"*The Relationship Advantage* is helping the CWWI salesforce transition from a reactive mode—responding to needs and requests—to a proactive selling organization that excels at anticipating customer requirements and collaborating with them to provide telecommunications solutions. This book provides a road map on how to succeed in a customer-driven marketplace with examples for understanding each customer's industry and business trends, for establishing strong business relationships with different levels in the organization, and for connecting the customer's business initiatives to high-value solutions."

—John Gregg, Executive Vice President Marketing Wireline Services, Cable & Wireless West Indies (CWWI)

"This book delivers wisdom from men of experience. The management team of every start-up should read this book as they prepare themselves to go to market. To be successful, the start-up has to be 'interested' not 'interesting.' As this book describes, they must 'go east.'"

—Tom Banahan, Global Head of Venture Capital, Lehman Brothers Venture Capital Group

"*The Relationship Advantage* is a compelling and important book. It is a timely one as well. Companies are struggling to improve salesforce performance while trying to figure out how to build and sustain customer relationships. This is perhaps the first book that offers a practical framework for relationship management, consultative selling, customer retention strategies, and the key role of the sales executive."

—Alf Henryk Wulf, Executive Vice President Sales and Marketing Europe, Alcatel

"Efficient service for customers, stimulating working environment for employees—Italgas Più works tirelessly toward guaranteeing this dual goal. We recognize that relationships with our customers and our people represent the keystone to business growth and service quality. Throughout *The Relationship Advantage* the message is crystal clear: Organizations that make their top priority deep relationships with their customers, suppliers, employees, and shareholders have a distinct advantage in any competitive marketplace."

—Cesare Cuniberto, General Manager, Italgas Più

"When all else is equal, people buy from people they like and trust. When all is not equal, people still try to buy from people they like and trust. *The Relationship Advantage* hits the mark in driving the knowledge required for enabling the consultative sale and the creation of loyal customers."

—Bryan L. Pickett, Vice President and General Manager, Global Knowledge Network Inc.

"The principles of *The Relationship Advantage* are powerful, the lessons are straightforward, and the offer of help is sincere. Tom and Sam were interested in our business and became trusted advisors for me. Relationships saved our firm when the Tech Bubble burst. Through key relationships in strategic accounts we experienced a 60 percent increase in sales last fiscal year."

—Jim Haskins, Senior Vice President of Client Services, Datatec Systems, Inc.

DEDICATION

To Julie, Allyson, T.J., and Debbie;
Patricia, Susan, Elizabeth, and Kevin

C *ontents*

Acknowledgments   ix

Introduction   xi

PART ONE
THE PARTNERSHIP CULTURE

1. TRUSTED ADVISORS   3

2. CONSULTING CULTURES   13

3. THE PYRAMID   23

4. MATCH ME IF YOU CAN   39

5. STEP UP TO VALUE   53

6. THE WHEEL OF FORTUNE   69

PART TWO
INTERPERSONAL ATTRIBUTES AND SKILLS

7. THE BIG THREE   87

8. THE BEST-KEPT SECRET   103

9. A MODEL ENGAGEMENT   109

10. QUESTIONS   123

11. GO EAST!   141

PART THREE
A PATH TO SUCCESS

12. DIAGNOSE AND PRESCRIBE   167

13. DON'T BID IF YOU CAN SELL   183

14. CRM—BLESSING OR CURSE?   193

15. FINAL THOUGHTS   205

Appendix A: Competency Profiles for Consultants   217
Appendix B: Creation Cycle Tactics 224
Appendix C: Identifying Consulting Prospects   227
Appendix D: Client Profile   231
Index   243

We would like to express our appreciation to all of the people who have supported us to this point on *The Relationship Advantage* journey, including thousands of the loyal members of IBM's client rep sales team, more than 4,000 members of Cisco Systems' global third-party channel organization, and many other sales organizations around the globe. We also appreciate and admire the many rainmakers we have known and emulated. Many thanks to Geoffrey Moore for his support and influence, and for his introduction to James Levine, whose contacts made this book possible; to Mary B. Good, Michael Cunningham, and Cynthia Zigmund at Dearborn for their education and patience; to all of our loyal friends and clients who said, "You guys ought to write a book"; and to Julie, my life partner, best friend, and advisor, for her critical eye and organizational ideas.

The decade of the 1990s saw unprecedented growth in practically every industry segment of the global economy. For many businesses, the keys to success were simply having enough of their products available for sale; keeping their distribution channels supplied; improving just-in-time production efficiency to produce large quantities of practically everything; increasing the number of sales personnel on the street and in telemarketing centers; and installing customer relationship management (CRM) computer systems to forecast sales demand. Customers and consumers didn't need to be sold. They bought! Many companies, especially those that provide technology products and services, adopted a build-it-and-they-will-come strategy. And it worked. Consumers and businesses raced to keep up with the siren call of the new economy. Many traditional business practices, including some accounting standards, were revised, creating new business practices and rules for the Internet revolution. Even blue chip companies like General Electric and IBM calculated executive bonuses based on their executives' ability to create viable Internet commerce strategies.

It's not surprising that this unprecedented rate of growth could not sustain itself. Indeed, scarcely two years into the new millennium, world financial markets were in disarray. All of the U.S.'s major financial market indices touched lows not seen for decades. Many who simply "built it" found that "they didn't come" after all. The dot-com bubble burst, and the fallout was devastating. Of course, the tragedy in New York on September 11, 2001, changed forever the way we will live and work.

THE BUBBLE'S IMPACT

Trust and confidence in our free enterprise system were challenged when the stock market bubble burst, leaving people stunned because so much trust was broken. Euphoria had driven several highly visible business leaders to think that the Internet revolution was an invitation to rewrite the book on business ethics. Several of these business icons were featured on television as they were dragged to jail in handcuffs by authorities, demonstrating a new dance step that newscasters called the "Perpetrator Walk!" Arthur Andersen, a beacon of auditing integrity for nearly a century, was forced to quit the audit profession over improprieties it committed when it stretched generally accepted accounting practices to help a handful of new economy clients. Providers of basic telephone and online services fought to survive the excesses of an infrastructure build-out that exceeded demand for their services. Banks discovered that their loan portfolios contained too many high-risk investments. Billions of dollars that were invested in high-tech and biotech start-ups during the boom of the 1990s were lost, and angry shareholders sued some of the premier stock brokerage firms and their analysts who had touted these new companies' initial public stock offerings. Pension funds and individual retirement plans suffered tremendous losses.

By 2003, people were not sure whom they could trust. Think for a moment. If you can't trust your banker, your lawyer, your broker, your retirement fund manager, your accountant, your telephone service, or the top executives that manage your place of employment, whom can you trust? Trust may take a lifetime to build, but it can be demolished in a single afternoon.

Those who felt betrayed by the financial and business institutions they had always trusted began modifying their behavior almost immediately. For example, venture capital funds cut back to almost zero the capital they were willing to invest in new economy ventures. Corporate expenditures budgeted for Internet commerce applications were scaled back to low levels, resulting in the extinction of many of the Internet revolution's high-flying application software and services companies. The leading providers of Internet commerce products, services, and software such as Cisco Systems, Sun Microsystems, Juniper Networks, Siebel Systems, PeopleSoft, Oracle, and many others were caught in the downward spiral and had to lay off thousands of workers.

When trust was broken, business owners, corporate leaders, executives, managers, and individual contributors began to approach their responsibilities with a healthy amount of caution. They became more analytical and began measuring many associates and suppliers on "templates of trust" they created to protect themselves. Business leaders who are burned once are not apt to let it happen again. Sales and marketing departments were the first to notice the impact when they discovered that it wasn't as easy to make quota as it had been in the 1990s. The Internet revolution had excused people from the need to invest in business relationships.

Have you created a personal trust template in your mind on which you rank associates, bosses, vendors, and others based on certain criteria you've constructed to protect yourself? Are you more analytical about making a commitment when suppliers ask you to sign the order? If you are in sales or marketing, have you noticed that sales cycles seem longer than you anticipated? If you joined the business world after 2003, have you noticed high—even extreme—levels of caution in your company's culture? Have you already discovered how important an ingredient trust is for most people when they are making decisions?

As you focus on the trustworthiness of others, remember to focus also on the flip side of the trust equation:

Other people are also ranking you on their *trust templates.*

This fact should prompt all of us to pause and reflect on the way we conduct ourselves in our business life. Trust is a two-way street. Do you know what attracts people to you, what makes you compelling at times? Do you know what people like or don't like about you? Are you considered trustworthy by those who are important to you? If so, do you know why they believe in you and trust your word? And if you are considered trustworthy, do you mentor those who don't share your good fortune and, perhaps, your habits and attributes?

To summarize, the 2000–2003 economic collapse broke our trust in many important ways, making us more cautious and less willing to trust people, processes, systems, and institutions. Business leaders and their salespeople now will have to conduct themselves and their business under a microscope. Earning their customers' trust, while difficult, will be the most essential ingredient in the mix if they want to grow and prosper in business.

WHY WRITE *THE RELATIONSHIP ADVANTAGE* AT THIS TIME?

We have spent the past 15 years mentoring executives and managers on how to create and maintain trust in their business relationships. This experience has taught us many lessons about the advantages that accrue from close business relationships. And it is these lessons that we want to pass along to our readers. The following statement seems self-evident, but read it carefully and think about it in the context of your organization's priorities:

> *Those organizations that make it a top priority to create deep relationships with their customers have a distinct advantage in their competitive marketplaces.*

Agree? Now, try the following statement on for size:

> *Few companies make building relationships with customers a top priority for the whole organization. Rather, most delegate it to the area in their organization that experiences the highest level of employee turnover—their salesforce.*

In this book we'll focus on the ways consulting partners create and maintain trusted relationships with their clients, showing in great detail how they mobilize their firms to participate in this pursuit. These methods are transferable to you. We have not seen many areas where trust is as important, yet so difficult for you to achieve, as in the day-to-day relationships with your customers.

You'll find this book is divided into three parts. In Part One, we present and discuss the attributes of consulting partnerships, focusing on their cultures and the unique ingredients that help consultants build trusted relationships with their clients. Part Two describes the interpersonal skills that facilitate consulting partners' success in building trusted client relationships. Part Three offers practical advice to those of you who want to improve the quality and depth of your relationship with your customers.

NATURAL ROLE MODELS

The best role models we have found for relationship building are the aforementioned partners in audit and consulting firms. These interesting, unassuming businesspeople have been creating trusted business relationships with their clients for years by behaving in ways that lead their clients to refer to them as "Trusted Advisors."

The recent demise of Arthur Andersen did not shake our confidence in these people. We asked four PricewaterhouseCoopers partners if they were excited about picking up Andersen's clients, and they expressed this unanimous sentiment: "Andersen's clients loved them, and they universally resent having to change their auditing relationships because a handful of bad apples spoiled the whole barrel!"

Through years of analysis and teaching, we have found that consulting partners' cultural attributes and processes can be taught to traditional businesspeople if they are open to learning new ways of doing business. *The Relationship Advantage*, a compendium of these processes and practices, has been presented to thousands of business leaders, managers, and individual contributors for the past 15 years, including IBM's vast global salesforce and Cisco Systems' global third-party network of channel partners. We have dedicated our business life to mentoring people in the ways of becoming trusted advisors.

The changes that we recommend to traditional business leaders and managers are both organizational and personal: *organizational* because successfully creating relationships must run to the core of any organization's values, meaning everyone at every level must accept accountability for creating and sustaining relationships. This accountability must not be delegated entirely to salesforces or other departments. Consulting firms are organized in a special way that enables all of the employees to participate in the building of client relationships. Although a consulting partnership's organizational structure is not a practical one to adopt for most traditional companies, many of the principles and processes found in partnerships will work for them. Our main goal in this book is to explain consulting partnership cultures, organizations, and processes so clearly that business organizations like yours can emulate them.

Regarding changes on a *personal* level, leaders and managers in traditional businesses are encouraged to recognize and appreciate the *interpersonal style* that allows consulting and audit partners to earn their clients' trust. Partners are the top-level managers in their firm, and they accept primary accountability for the quality of their firm's relationships with, and satisfaction of, their clients. They refer to their customers as "clients." We'll explore the differences between being customer focused and client focused with you in this book. By the way, many of the behaviors that appear to be client focused are often at odds with the tactical requirements of most businesses—like this week's forecast. Consulting and audit partners approach their clients in ways that create and build trust, and they understand that building trust is a marathon, not a sprint. It is strategic, not tactical. It takes time. The interpersonal nature, style, and cultural attributes of consulting and audit partners are genuine, unlike many of the manipulative selling techniques employed by most businesses to ensure short-term sales orders and other business results.

Even though we always found that businesses could benefit from understanding these processes and attributes, we believe the need for understanding them has never been greater than it is today, given the high degree of misplaced trust that exists. Mutual trust is hard to come by these days. Many of your customers are hesitant to make long-term commitments to suppliers—new or old. Aren't you?

Building trust is largely a matter of the heart, something all of us have been taught to leave out of business. *The Relationship Advantage* is designed to help you put the heart back into your business culture if you'll allow it to happen. Business conducted from the heart in a trustworthy fashion will lead to trusted relationships. Those who learn to establish trust will be tomorrow's market leaders, leaving others to follow in their dust. Adoption of these ideas by traditional businesses will require a large amount of change, change that must first be adopted by executives and top-level managers. Those of you at the top will be challenged to lead your employees and customers by your own example. We can think of no pursuit more important at this time. We hope you're up to the challenge.

Part One

THE PARTNERSHIP CULTURE

1

TRUSTED ADVISORS

Trust opens the door to the spirit!

Have you noticed how many businesses seem to struggle with creating and maintaining enduring relationships with their customers? The Internet became an overnight success in improving communication between suppliers and their customers. But, as with all technology solutions, the Internet cannot be expected to create relationships. When maximized for internal use, Internet solutions only help businesses forecast, calculate, and measure their performance.

A high percentage of the senior business managers and leaders we have met agree that relationship building requires people-to-people interaction. Yet they have spent billions of dollars on Web-based tools for customer relationship management (CRM) that are authored and marketed by technology leaders like Oracle, Siebel Systems, PeopleSoft, and IBM. These leaders have also invested billions of dollars in various sales training programs such as Spin Selling and PSS from Xerox; Customer Oriented Selling at IBM; Strategic Selling from Miller-Heiman; Target Account Selling by Siebel; Power Base Selling from Holden; and literally hundreds of similar sales process providers. In addition, companies have made substantial financial investments and have committed more of their precious information systems resources in trying to automate these sales training programs and link them to their CRM systems.

Shouldn't all of this investment in software and automated training systems have yielded a consensus—a best practices methodology for building relationships with customers—by now? We know that kind of consensus has not been reached because most companies are still making new commitments every year to new sales training programs. Salesforces refer to this indecision and lack of commitment by their top managers as "sales training du jour!" There's always been a tendency to look for a silver bullet, in this case a prepackaged and guaranteed technique for building trusted relationships. How much more investment will be required to convince business leaders that, when it comes to building relationships, there is no silver bullet?

Incorporating frequent changes in a company's selling process works against the goal of building relationships because each change in the sales process introduces new ways of dealing with customers. This causes "relationship interruptis" while salespeople try to figure out what their management is telling them this year about how they are expected to deal with their customers. This recipe for disaster is exacerbated when companies decide to reassign customers and sales territories (a frequent occurrence in most companies we've known) in the midst of all of the retraining. These concurrent activities almost ensure that long-term, strategic relationships will not be possible to cultivate. What's going on here? Or, as our teenagers are fond of saying, "What's up with that?"

We believe if a company is to achieve "the relationship advantage," it must force itself to take a fresh look at the actions and behaviors that will create strategic, lasting customer relationships. Such a company can benefit tremendously by looking objectively at the culture, processes, and organizational structures in consulting partnerships. The communication styles and interpersonal behaviors of the partners, senior managers, and staff members who manage the client relationships in these firms should also be studied. Consulting firms possess the relationship advantage and so will you after you follow us into the inner workings of these professional firms, where you will discover many techniques and processes that have never before been documented.

EASY TO SAY, HARD TO DO

Corporate leaders and their team members who want to build trusted relationships with their customers will have to make dramatic changes in the way they approach their customers. Those of you who marvel at the ease with which consulting and audit partners achieve true business partner status with their clients' management teams will finally learn how and why they are able to do it.

Little has been written about the inner workings of professional partnerships, a fact that alone has caused these simple processes and attributes to take on an almost mythical quality. As is the case with so many legendary and mysterious things, these powerful partnership attributes are rooted in common sense.

Successful implementation of these powerful ideas will only be possible if those of you who are leaders and top managers are willing to redefine the role you personally play with your customers. You have to accept personal accountability for creating and managing customer relationships, accountability you have traditionally delegated to others, most frequently to your salesforces.

TRUST

The word *trust* is derived from the German word *trost*, which means comfort. It implies instinctive, unquestioning belief in, and reliance on, something. *The American Heritage Dictionary* (New College ed.) provides a simple definition:

> Trust: *A firm reliance on the integrity, ability, or character of a person or thing; a confident belief; a faith*

Think how important trust is to you in every aspect of your life. Whom do you trust? Why? What leads you to trust people? Just as important, what leads people to trust you? Can you identify with certainty the trusted relationships you have in business? How about those in your personal life? What qualities come to mind that caused you to categorize relationships this way?

Most of us take trust for granted in our daily transactions with employees, suppliers, shareholders, and customers. Being perceived as trustworthy is an assumed element in our business relationships. Trustworthiness promotes good business results, whereas its lack can kill potential relationships, both in business and in our personal life. Perhaps we get in such a comfortable groove with our assumptions about trust that we don't pay enough attention to it. *One of our goals is to help you understand how you can enable your customers to recognize your trustworthiness.* Your personal relationships may benefit from a trust tune-up as well.

Understanding the important role trust plays in our best business relationships is the first step in creating trusted relationships. Trust is subjective and personal, because our trust is given or withheld based more on our perceptions than on reality. Trust makes it unnecessary to examine motives, to look for hidden meanings, to "have it in writing," to have someone like a lawyer intervene in a relationship to ensure understanding. If trust is missing, we are less open, less interdependent. We look for strategies to deal with each other at the same time we seek protection in rules, contracts, and the law.

The level of trust in a relationship is the thermometer of the relationship's health. How often have you thought, "I'm not sure why, but I just don't trust that person"? Perhaps your feelings in such cases are influenced by the other individual's personal style. Consider some of the selling styles you have observed where stereotypes have emerged—some deserved and some not. Certain salespeople are known to employ sales processes that are predictable, sometimes insulting, and often comical. Consider the actions of the often-maligned automobile salesperson who always wants to "give you an incredible deal if you'll buy right now, because the boss wants to sell this car today." The salesperson proposes to "write up your offer for you, tell you how much to offer, take your offer to the boss, and see if he'll accept it." It is seldom a surprise to find out that "the boss wants a little more money than you're offering!"

No wonder some auto companies have introduced a no-negotiation policy for new cars. But the game continues year after year. These hardworking salespeople aren't bad people; they're only trying to make a living, so we don't resent them on a personal level. They are simply driven by a tactical process that is designed to help them make a short-term sale. *The process is not designed to earn your trust!* Auto salespeople know that if you don't buy right now, on impulse, they'll never see you again, but if you *do* buy, they won't see you again for three years at a minimum. This is most likely the process that makes you distrust the salesperson. Surely your own selling process is better than this one. But how much better? Are you making sales and creating solid relationships at the same time? Or are you only making short-term, tactical sales while treating every opportunity as if it's your last gasp before the prospect walks away?

Until the turn of the new millennium, selling was relatively easy; that is, easy compared with how it works today. In the great economic boom of the 1980s and 1990s, those who sold technology products, for example, found their major issue wasn't finding prospects who wanted to buy their products. The issue was keeping supply levels high enough to fulfill demand. Many companies like Cisco, Dell, Hewlett-Packard, and IBM had to sell large quantities of their products through third-party channel partners and telemarketing centers because their direct salesforces were literally out of breath satisfying demand for their products. Today, most of those high-flying companies are rediscovering that, like the traditional old economy companies, they now have to take a more active role in touching their end customers again as they compete for their piece of a slower-growing pie.

Our purpose is not to dwell on the past or on the amount of trust that has been broken. Rather, we want to define the current playing field regarding the status of vendor-customer relationship building so that we can offer an alternative pathway to help you understand the importance of trust, learn how to build it, and infuse it into the relationships you value most. To participate in this process, you must be willing to suspend many beliefs that have previously been ingrained in you in your traditional business training.

The biggest of these mistaken beliefs constantly reminds you that your most endearing personal behaviors, traits, and feelings don't belong in business. "Don't get personal about this," or "Leave your personal life at the door when you enter the office," and "Keep friendships separate from business" are beliefs that have derailed many potential business relationships. Nowhere has this been felt as dramatically as in the arena of customer relationships.

Mention customer relationships and the subject of sales training jumps into the foreground. Nowhere in business have we done a greater disservice to young, high-potential people as in the various sales training and performance programs we've offered them during the past half century.

Thousands of professional sales trainers have taught salespeople that potential customers can be manipulated into ordering products. This manipulation is always hidden in a process whereby customers are led through a series of steps that supposedly will prompt them to "sign the order." Although a certain amount of this type of training is credible in some situations that we discuss later, we want to establish our bias right now:

MANIPULATION DOES NOT BUILD TRUST.

Manipulation is contrary to trust, and trust is the foundation on which meaningful relationships are built. If you don't believe that, you're reading the wrong book. Think how you feel when you know someone is trying to manipulate you when you're buying a car, listening to an investment idea, or attempting to choose the best political candidate. Doesn't manipulation make you want to turn and run in the opposite direction? What do these experiences tell you about trusting people who try to manipulate you?

SALES TRAINING

Our extensive experience with many of the most popular sales training programs shows that most of them are based on one basic architectural scheme. Designers of sales training curricula used to call this architectural scheme FBR: Feature–Benefit–Reaction. Many of the more recently created programs hide this scheme in as many as a dozen steps, augmented with such procedures as empathy building, effective questioning, listening, benefit analysis, and others too numerous to mention. They also require sales reps to do a lot of recordkeeping and clerical work; and each program comes with its own set of documentation requirements for sales reps to complete as a part of the process. Because the documents created by training companies aren't compatible with CRM systems, sales reps are forced to handle duplicate paperwork requirements.

FBR-based processes assume that sales reps have managed to get in front of a prospect to present their wares, a fallacious assumption given the difficulty most sales reps have securing appointments with the right individuals. Once they've managed to get in front of a customer, sales reps are instructed to start what amounts to a monologue by executing an IBS, or Initial Benefit Statement. An IBS is supposed to be an attention grabber that will make the customer sit up and take notice. Here's an example of an IBS:

> Sales rep: *Thank you for making time on your busy calendar for me this morning. I am confident that when I am through describing our offerings, you will see why all of your competitors have switched to the product I am going to show you this morning! Sound good so far? Then let me get started.*

The FBR monologue is executed immediately after the IBS in a fashion that looks something like this:

> Feature: *I am excited to present to you our _____ (product), which is the latest and most effective product in our family of products. Unlike previous models, it does x, y, and z!*
> Benefit: *Our customers have experienced many benefits as a result of owning the _____ (product). The main benefits they have received are (1) _____, (2) _____, and (3)_____.*
> Reaction: *Now that you understand the benefits of this exciting new product, what is your reaction to what I've presented?*

That nice, tight process is ideal for presenting products or services when a sales rep has been invited to present a bid. Even though bidding is a necessary evil of doing business in many cases, it also means that the bidder has not assumed the initiative in constructing the deal. He or she is only able to react or respond to requirements that are someone else's creation. Trust is not an issue in bidding because there is little room for trust to develop when you're fighting for an order. We acknowledge that bidding is often necessary, but our emphasis in this book is on creating the kinds of relationships that preclude bidding.

The selling processes that we reference here also include techniques designed to help sales reps overcome objections and rejection when they receive a negative answer to the "what's your reaction" question. The best known and most frequently used of these techniques is called

FFF: Feel–Felt–Found. The following example of a shopworn FFF statement shows how your sales reps have been coached to respond to negative reactions:

> Sales rep: *Mr./Ms. Prospect, I understand how you* feel! *Many of our
> customers have* felt *exactly the same way at first. But after using our
> product, they have* found *profitable outcomes and (on and on).*

This is not criminal behavior. In fact, this is what people who are in
the market for goods and services have come to expect. But is this kind
of behavior sincere? Is it manipulative? Does it engender trust? How do
you like it when someone you don't know says to you, "I know how you
feel"? If you are a top-level manager and one of these people slips through
your screen, do you spend time with him or her?

What's wrong with saying "I know how you feel"? What's wrong is
that *you don't know* how the other person feels. Worse, the person knows
you don't know! Statements and techniques like this have worked their
way into every traditional business organization we have seen. Their
value is best realized in the inevitable bidding situations that arise. The
problem is that sales executives, managers, and reps revert to these behaviors because they know them and feel comfortable using them regardless of the opportunity or venue. Don't you? The result is that
meetings that could be used for developing relationships default automatically to an **FBR-FFF** contest because these learned techniques prompt
habitual responses from both sales rep and customer.

TRUSTED ADVISORS

Consulting and audit partners, on the other hand, behave differently,
in ways that are 180 degrees from traditional sales methods. Because we
consider consulting and audit partners role models, we'll build a profile
of their attributes so that you can see how their unique behaviors bring
them profitable results from clients who consider them Trusted Advisors.

When clients look at a consulting partner as a potential Trusted Advisor, they are thinking, "Is this someone I can trust? Is this someone I
can share my concerns with? Is this someone who will solve problems
and not create new ones?" Clients who have issues and problems are

looking for advisors who exhibit authentic behavior—meaning advisors who bring focus to these three outcomes:

1. Establishing collaborative relationships
2. Solving problems so they stay solved
3. Working concurrently on both the business problem and the relationship (personal) issues

From Consultant to Trusted Advisor

A few years ago Sam Barcus was providing financial and management consulting services for a 100-year-old family-owned dairy in New Orleans. After traveling to New Orleans every other week over a two-year period, Sam had become an ad hoc member of the senior management team. His primary client contact was the chairman-CEO, a third-generation family member who had taken over the reins from his father. During the first year of the assignment, most of Sam's time was spent with the chairman discussing financial and business issues. As they moved into the second year of the relationship, they would often have dinner together; and, increasingly, their discussions moved beyond the day-to-day issues within the company.

According to Sam, "A particularly unique aspect of family-owned businesses is their desire to hand off the company to another family member. The chairman had three children, but no matter how much he persisted, none of his children was really interested in taking over the family business."

Sam continues, "One day, late into the second year of the assignment, I got a call from the chairman with a special request. We talked about his frustration that none of his children wanted to follow in his footsteps, and then he brought up the reason for the call. His nephew had approached him about learning the dairy business and eventually taking over the company. In the next moment I fully understood the weightiness of being a Trusted Advisor. The chairman asked if I would interview his nephew and let him know if I thought his nephew should be invited in to learn the business. The 'light bulb' went off for me as I realized that my relationship with the chairman had gone well beyond providing financial and business consultation to providing advice about personal—and personnel—matters relating to the family business—truly the role of a Trusted Advisor."

Authentic behavior leads to higher trust, higher leverage, and higher client commitment.

You might invite FBR and FFF people into your evaluation process when you are seeking bids for products to build a solution that you have defined, probably with the help of your consultant or auditor. But would you trust a practitioner of FBR and FFF to give you advice on the mission-critical issues for your business? If not, where would you go to get such advice? Most business leaders' responses to this question that we've heard were summarized beautifully by one of our clients who said:

> *Salespeople appear when* they *need something, so I see a lot of them buzzing around here at the end of every month and every quarter. Consultants, on the other hand, seem to be here when* I *need something! I prefer to see the consultants.*

We have concluded that people will regard you as a Trusted Advisor when you give them good advice. The question: How do you do that with customers' executives whom you've not met? The answer: Consultants make it their business to know their customers' executives. That's why we'll devote the rest of this book to explaining how they do it—how and why they become Trusted Advisors. We are not proposing that you should become a consultant. Instead, we want you to see how consultants approach their customers and why they refer to them as "clients." We hope you discover ways to modify your behavior and that of your team members so you will become Trusted Advisors to your customers.

SUMMARY

Now is a good time for traditional business managers and leaders to take a fresh look at how they prioritize and build relationships with their customers. Traditional selling methods, designed for bidding products, are not appropriate for building trust, which is the cornerstone of relationships. Partners in consulting firms are strong role models for those business leaders who want to improve the quality of their customer relationships. Following these partners' examples requires business leaders to reassess their personal role within their own organization—especially the role they play with their customers.

2

CONSULTING CULTURES

The cultural attributes that are exhibited by employees at all levels within consulting firms can serve as a guide for you and your organization to help put you on your way to creating trusted relationships. This applies to you if you are a CEO, VP, director, sales rep, or staff member in a traditional business. What makes consulting firms and their partners tick? Let's begin by considering what consulting is all about, because the nature of a business determines the nature of the people within it. Here are five characteristics that generally define consulting.

1. **Independent orientation.** Executives within your organization, as well as those in your customers' businesses, often feel the need to discuss issues and problems with people whom they perceive to be dispassionate or objective. The key word here is *perceive*. We know that no one is truly objective. People who are frustrated day in and day out with their inability to solve problems tend to get into ruts, become blind to new approaches to old problems, and find it impossible to be objective about the problems. Top executives often tell us that their own staff members tend to tell them what they want to hear, not what they really think. People often feel that telling the boss the truth may rock the boat, especially

when the truth brings bad news, so they continue on the path they've always pursued. This brings to mind the once popular definition of *insanity:*

Insanity: *Expecting to achieve different results by doing the same things*

Executives who use outside, objective experts when they need help created an old expression that is commonly associated with consultants: "You have to be from out of town to be an expert." Whether the perception of objectivity is true or false, it is often easier to define and solve a problem when we're not personally involved, and consultants fit that description because they exist outside the client's sphere of influence.

Another less obvious reason why executives bring in outsiders is that they feel embarrassed about asking for help. Unloading on a stranger can be a way to alleviate pain while saving face within their organizations.

2. Special training and qualifications. A second commonly held perception is that consultants attend some sort of secret training school where they learn how to help people. It *is* true that they receive continuing education within their firm. Would you be surprised to learn that consulting partners receive the bulk of this training from their clients on the job? Yes, clients pay consultants to learn about clients' businesses. And consultants learn by listening to their clients' issues and problems, and through collaborating with clients on solutions.

Consultants know that a client will find the right solution to his or her problem when properly assisted in finding it. Naturally, the consultants who boast the best reputations are known for giving the best advice regarding specific issues and problems. They and their employees specialize in solving problems in such areas, among many others, as salesforce development, logistics, manufacturing, human resources, total quality management, and compensation. Years of positive experience with a multitude of clients within a specialized area enhance the credibility and resulting reputation of these specialized firms and their individual practitioners. The consultants gain more and more confidence in their ability to provide advice every time they complete an engagement; and each engagement teaches them more about their area of specialization.

Though we have been taught not to confuse our personal experiences with business, most of us have accumulated valuable experience that can be applied to customer situations from helping friends or family members in discussions about problems or crises. Often, the appropriate solution was obvious, and a friend merely needed someone to help expose it.

We are able to help people when we know them, take the time to listen, understand their issue, and care enough to work through it with them. And we don't require any special training or qualifications to do that. The person with the problem teaches us all we need to know about it, and we can brainstorm solutions from the shared understanding we reach through our dialogue. If the person provides us with bad information that negatively affects our understanding of the issue, then he or she bears responsibility for the outcome. And that's the way consulting works as well. A consultant's solution can be only as accurate and effective as the input received from the person with the problem.

3. Personal references. To whom do you turn when you are seeking advice in your personal life? A friend? Partner? Clergyman? Therapist? Spouse? Whether you look for advice often or seldom, you probably agree that when you turn to someone, you turn to someone you believe you can trust. Most of us wouldn't run to a local fortune-teller or tarot card reader, nor would we trust our horoscope.

Executives often seek the advice of consultants but not those they find in the Yellow Pages or in newspaper advertisements. Most consulting business—90 percent or more—occurs through *personal references*. Consultants trade heavily on their credibility, and they are usually approached because of their reputation. One of the most difficult things to do in traditional selling is to call on someone you don't know and have never met, an activity that sales reps refer to as a "cold call." Consulting partners don't make cold calls, because they are *referred* to new clients, which is much more efficient than cold calling and significantly raises the odds for a successful meeting.

4. Problem identification and problem solving. The greatest value provided by consultants is problem solving. Tangible, successful consulting results depend on more than an objective point of view, special training, and a good reputation. They also depend on a consultant's ability to lead clients through proven processes that produce positive results; clients insist they want bulletproof problem-solving techniques.

There are two distinct phases in problem solving: A problem must first be diagnosed before it can be solved. It stands to reason that problems cannot be solved until they are understood. (We discuss problem solving in great detail in Chapter 12.)

Effectively diagnosing problems requires consultants to maintain a clear, almost maniacal focus on their clients' issues. In Chapter 11, we show you how to use a simple compass as an effective metaphor for describing the directional focus exhibited by consultants during their conversations with clients regarding business issues.

Let's return for a moment to the typical FBR-FFF salesperson. Over the past several years, salespeople have received many upgrades to their basic sales education, the most prevalent of which teaches sales reps to represent themselves as *solution providers*. The FBR devotee has been coached to say, "I'm here today to present our XYZ solution." We think salespeople would do well to heed this simple concept:

To have a solution, there must be a problem.

Nowhere are solutions more abundant than in the high-tech arena. IBM marketed its Risc 6000 solutions against Sun Microsystems' Sparc server solutions in a classic matchup of competitive products. These two companies were fortunate that the Internet had built so much momentum that businesses jumped on these solutions without considering the *problem* they solved!

Cisco Systems provides a specific example of how customers sometimes don't go along with a supplier's attempt to position a product as a *solution*. Cisco had developed a controller that allows businesses to connect their telephones to the Internet, saving long-distance phone tariffs and allowing computer applications to be run concurrently with phone calls. Sales reps were taught to present this exciting new controller as the Voice over IP Solution to their prospects. Predictably, most business managers who weren't trying to reduce long-distance charges or trying to run phones concurrently with Internet applications didn't respond favorably to presentations about Cisco's solution. As a result, the product didn't garner the initial enthusiasm Cisco had forecast.

Had Cisco taken the time to assist those customers through a business process evaluation that unearthed cost implications and inefficiencies of running phones and applications separately, then the targeted customers may have viewed Cisco's product as a solution. Since that time, Cisco has developed a consultative group called IBSG—Internet Business Solutions Group—that works with select customers, facilitating a business process evaluation for them before recommending products. This is a step ahead for Cisco, but the IBSG continues its work far from the mainstream sales team.

Traditional sales managers possess neither the patience nor the skill-sets necessary to provide their customers with the right kind of problem identification and problem-solving assistance. Many seem unaware that their customers need to first understand their problems, before they will purchase a product or service. This puts most vendor organizations at a disadvantage when their customers seek help with the primary step of analysis. Salespeople who are eager to make quota and sell their products with great efficiency usually *relinquish their diagnosis and analysis opportunities to consultants.*

Delegating problem diagnosis and analysis to others spoils the best opportunity salespeople have early on to initiate actions that lead to trusted relationships. Sales reps have told us with great consistency that their customers, when faced with the need to perform analysis, often tell them, "Look, we'll do this analysis, and we'll consider calling you when we know what we need."

5. Keeping promises (a services mind-set). One of the things that haunts consultants is not knowing beyond a shadow of a doubt that they are making a difference, not knowing that their consulting engagement is really adding value to a client's situation and resolving a critical issue or problem. Consulting at its best is an act of caring. It calls for a sincere desire to be genuinely helpful to a client by using knowledge and experience—often gained through specialization—to improve the client's situation. Consulting cannot be done well without a genuine caring for the client, caring that is demonstrated by the way promises are made—and kept.

The elements that make up the foundation of a successful client-consultant relationship are twofold: First is the consultant's ability to diagnose the problem; second is the client's acceptance of the consultant's promise to resolve the problem. Sustaining the relationship is based on the consultant building deeper trust and credibility by fulfilling the promise.

Successfully diagnosing the problem requires the ability to understand and appreciate the client's current business issues and initiatives. This involves aligning the consultant's capabilities with the client's initiatives and then defining what's known as a *promise of satisfaction*. This is an informal agreement in which the consultant spells out orally—and the client hears—what will be delivered. Coming to grips with the things that are of interest and importance to the client and then jointly deciding how to go forward generates both confidence and interest in developing the relationship. Each step along the way establishes an *agreement in principle* with the client that helps manage expectations and strengthens the commitment to proceed. When working with clients on these promises, *successful consultants underpromise and overdeliver.*

Confronting substantive business issues is one of the most difficult tasks of the consulting process. When the process works perfectly, the client says, "We have an issue. Here it is. How do we solve it?" Unfortunately, this doesn't happen often because the client doesn't understand the issue or is unwilling to address it. Uncovering real issues requires the consultant to possess the ability to listen to the spoken words, thoughts, and emotions that are behind the words. Only by listening with sincere interest can the consultant identify the true issues and establish a promise of satisfaction to resolve the issue.

This promise, or tacit agreement, is established, built, and affirmed on a cluster of expectations, impressions, and perceptions formed through various encounters with the consultant. A key part of this process is helping the client reduce uncertainty, thus increasing the client's confidence and peace of mind. The client plays an important role by helping to define the promise and by establishing practical boundaries around the solution possibilities that arise in the collaboration with the consultant. The client is heavily influenced through interacting with the consultant in many ways—meetings, correspondence, documents, presentations, and discussions with colleagues.

CUSTOMER OR CLIENT

The five characteristics listed above differentiate consultants and their cultures from the businesses and business leaders that they serve. In a nutshell, traditional businesses make a product, then sell it, and finally install or implement it. This make–sell–implement business cycle is fundamental to every traditional business we've seen.

Consultants, however, modify that business cycle in a dramatic way. They use their diagnostic processes and skills to *sell* a solution to fit the diagnosed production problem as the first step in their process; then they figure out how to *make* the product; and finally they *implement* it.

The traditional business practice—make–sell—is the generally accepted way companies bring their products into the marketplace. These products are usually hard goods that offer little or no chance for modification or customization. In this world, a product is what it is and should be sold "as is."

The consulting business practice—sell–make—offers almost unlimited opportunities for customization; sell–make is the generally accepted way in which consultants work with their clients. The difference between these two approaches (traditional and consulting business) provides many clues to the difference between treatment as a *customer* and treatment as a *client*. Can you see how these two very different approaches to business and the huge behavioral differences they imply create distinctly different impressions within the mind of the customer or client being served?

The traditional business makes a product as the first step and then has to sell volumes of that product to survive and grow the business. It's no surprise that traditional marketing organizations meet this challenge by trying to position their products as "solutions" to customers who have no frame of reference for why they need them. A supplier's salespeople have to hustle to present their products, leaving little or no time for understanding a customer's issues. It's caveat emptor—let the buyer beware!

Contrast that traditional product-marketing scenario with a typical consulting engagement. Consultants invest the time to diagnose a client's issue as the first step in their sales process. They gather detailed data, clearly define the problem, and then sell a solution. There is no need to present features and benefits because the product hasn't been made yet. All of the focus on the client's issues allows empathy to develop naturally, and the consultant and client get to know each other very well. Once the solution is sold, consultants make that *customized solution* for the client.

The fundamental difference between customers and clients is that the primary task with a *customer* is to sell a product already made. The job with a *client* is to serve his or her needs, which may mean that the product will be included in the customized solution the consultants make. Customers purchase products from sales reps, whereas clients collaborate with consultants to make solutions. Sales reps begin their presentations with products (FBR), whereas consultants treat products as items to be budgeted in a custom solution. Both of these alternative positions are deeply rooted in the cultures of the two kinds of businesses. *Moving a company's focus from customer to client requires a firm understanding of both business and consulting cultures. That's what the rest of this book will cover.*

We'll close this discussion about consulting attributes with the following true story. The subject happens to be technology, but any type of product could be inserted for the story to work. You will note how the actions of the salesman and his manager cement their reputation as vendors, not trusted advisors. Although they don't follow the FBR recipe completely, you'll notice that they do lead with a presentation about themselves during their first encounter with a key customer executive. We think this scenario has a ring of familiarity with our readers.

T h e   B a n k e r

I was mentoring a group of about 500 IBM salespeople and systems support people in Montreal as part of the client rep program we conducted for thousands of IBM's employees. In our experience, people seldom raise their hands to speak in a session so large, but I had apparently hit a nerve with my assertion that salespeople are not perceived to be trusted advisors because they usually focus on their own agenda, often talking when they should be asking questions and listening to the customer's responses.

On this day, however, a young IBM salesman did raise his hand in the middle of the auditorium and, in a delightful French accent, said something like this:

> *May I please speak? Last week my boss and I met with the president of the largest bank in Quebec. It took us months to get an appointment with this executive. Once we scheduled the appointment, we cleared our calendars so we could work on the presentation.*

The red flag was raised for me already. What could they possibly present to an executive they had never met? He continued:

When we arrived in this gentleman's office, we found that his secretary, as promised, had set up an overhead projector and screen for us. We thanked the president for taking time out of his busy schedule to see us and then we jumped right into the presentation. The CEO was very cordial and polite during our 30-minute presentation. After the meeting, the two of us celebrated our accomplishment. After all, we had just spent half an hour with one of the most influential executives in all of Canada!

Naturally, I had to ask why he needed to tell all of us this story.

Your discussion about Trusted Advisors just made me realize something. I don't have a reason to go back to see this man again! You see, my boss and I told him everything we know about banking! And we told him everything we know about his bank and everything we know about IBM! We also told him how many customers IBM has worldwide in banking! But we never asked him a single question! *We didn't even ask him if he had an opinion about the wisdom of spending the $3 million his bank spent with IBM over the past year on a new teller system. Now I am embarrassed by our actions. The CEO certainly knows more about his bank and the general subject of banking than we will ever know. Unless he's a big stockholder, he's probably not very interested in IBM. It's like we had a loaded pistol, and we fired every one of our bullets into the man. There's no telling what we could have learned if we had just asked him some questions.*

I asked what the CEO said as they left the meeting and he responded: "Good review. Maybe we'll see you again next year!" Here's the lesson we hope you'll take away from this story:

Don't give a presentation unless you're certain that the information you are presenting is appropriate to the needs of the audience.

If this were your customer, would "Maybe we'll see you again next year" be a satisfactory conclusion to this meeting? How does this example stack up to other experiences you may have had in the recent past?

How do your sales teams conduct themselves when they finally earn an appearance before the CEO of a key customer account?

SUMMARY

Consulting cultures differ from those of traditional businesses in many ways. Consultants thrive as a result of clients' perceptions of consultants' effectiveness—the most commonly held perception being that consultants are purely objective in their orientation. Rather than learning their trade in classrooms, consultants are mentored on the job. This means that clients, unwittingly, often pay their consultants to learn the clients' business. Thus, the skills and business acumen exhibited by consultants are often learned through experience, not formal education.

Rather than conducting cold canvassing campaigns to garner new clients, consultants obtain the great majority of their new engagements from personal references. Their irrepressible focus on their clients' issues endears consultants to their clients who, in turn, are most happy to refer the consultants to others. The deep, trusting relationships that result from their ability to solve problems are the lifeblood of successful consulting firms.

C h a p t e r

3

THE PYRAMID

The sales team in the banker story that was reported in Chapter 2 performed according to the expectations that most executives we've interviewed say they have when sales representatives from one of their vendors invite them to a sales presentation. Is it any wonder that with this kind of conditioning, executives are so hard to approach? If you are an executive or if you function at any other level of management within your company, do you look for opportunities to engage with your suppliers' salespeople? Do you tend to trust them implicitly and unconditionally? Would you seek out a vendor's salespeople to provide advice on your critical business issues?

Assuming that you answered no to these questions, here's another question that you and most other executives have not considered: Do you think that the executives who run your customers' organizations want to spend their time with *your* salespeople?

FIRST-STRIKE ENGAGEMENT

The shape of traditional business organization charts has changed somewhat as technology has improved productivity for most workers at

23

P o p   Q u i z

1. *Does your company measure and recognize salespeople based on their ability to call on top managers and executives?*

2. *Did your career begin in sales? If so, were you effective at calling on executives? Were you able to create and manage trusted relationships with decision makers?*

3. *Does your sales executive complain about the inability of your sales organization to call high enough in your customers' organizations?*

4. *Do you expect that your customers will regard your salespeople more highly than you regard theirs?*

5. *If you are an executive, department head, or any other type of general manager, what are the specific things that you do to assume accountability for relationships with key customers?*

all levels of management. Even so, most businesses remain hierarchical. Businesses adopted hierarchical organizations starting with the Industrial Revolution at the beginning of the 20th century, and these patterns became the norm after the two great wars of that century. Looking at a generic organization chart, perhaps your own company's chart, it is easy to superimpose a military structure on top of it. The term *chain of command,* often used in business discussions, came from the military, and the chain analogy became the generally accepted way to get things done in business organizations as well.

Consider the army: Generals and colonels, like CEOs and other top executives, have responsibility for strategy and overall direction. Majors, like department heads and vice presidents, provide linkage from the strategists to the tactical people who live in the trenches. Next in line as we roll down the chain of command are captains, who are comparable to department or business area directors. Captains command the day-to-day tactical resources in battle in much the same way as your company's branch and regional managers look for ways to achieve quota points. Next down the line are first and second lieutenants, the first management-level people to be involved in battle who are much like your sales and customer support managers. At the bottom, of course, are soldiers. They are analogous to your individual contributors, such as service technicians, sales reps, factory workers, and so on. These "soldiers" execute the fundamental tasks required to accomplish the business of their respective companies.

In these traditional structures, the ability to delegate responsibility and authority is a treasured characteristic. Haven't we all heard the old wartime jokes about top military commanders telling their troops, "Go get 'em, boys! We'll be observing you through heavy lenses from that mountaintop over there!"

Top-level corporate managers, acting in the capacity of generals and colonels, prefer to send individual contributors—soldiers—to acquire tactical targets. Consulting partners, on the other hand, don't do that; they make themselves personally accountable for acquiring business for their firms. That's what it means to be a partner, and, as you're about to discover, a partnership's organizational methods tip traditional business organizations upside down.

The executives from supplier and customer organizations who participate in business deals typically wait to meet each other until the deal is won or lost and one of them has submitted to the other. But partners meet and engage their client executives at the first strike. If you are a top executive, how often do you engage with your peers from your customers' and suppliers' organizations? Do you engage at the beginning of a deal? Do you lead the first strike, or do you wait until the action has stopped, delegating the first strike to your soldiers? Let's see how most companies that delegate first strikes put themselves at a disadvantage when they're introducing new products.

SALES QUOTAS VERSUS STRATEGY

Imagine you have identified a market opportunity that can make or break your company. You have defined the opportunity, developed new products or services as prototypes, and put your control systems in place; and now your marketing group is ready to promote the new product or service. You have also identified 20 potential users for this new product. Early acceptance by these 20 customers is needed to ensure success. Ready to get the ball rolling?

How will you start the dialogue with the 20 strategic companies whose support you need to ensure success? Have you figured out the level in the 20 organizations at which your idea must be presented in order to sell it? Who are the people in the 20 companies that you know well enough to trust with this opportunity, and who among them trusts you enough to take the risk to help you? Are these people working at the level you have targeted? Are they generals, colonels, or majors? Who will schedule the first strike with them?

Do you see how important *trust* is in this equation? We're really asking, "Do you have 20 *trusted relationships*?" Most businesses don't. Typically, a company's soldiers are expected to make these initial, first-strike contacts. But the problem is that soldiers usually engage other soldiers who work at their same administrative or operational levels, not at the levels where strategic alliances and partnerships originate—where the "war" is planned. Whereas soldiers acquire tactical targets, sales reps' motivation is quota attainment, but they are seldom able to invest the time and resources required to direct and manage strategic initiatives.

Sales reps are paid to be tactical, and they survive by achieving their weekly, monthly, and quarterly sales quotas. It is rare to find a sales rep willing to forgo his or her pay and recognition in order to make a strategic contribution, unless management has waived tactical milestones and co-opted the sales rep into helping. Here's a tongue-in-cheek description of salespeople: "Lousy sales reps have skinny kids!" Salespeople have to feed their kids, and making strategic calls that lack the potential to produce high sales volumes doesn't put bread on the table.

THE MISSING LINK

Nothing happens in most companies until something's sold. Your sales reps dutifully call on their customers and record the pertinent data from their sales calls—hoping they include lots of sales orders—into your CRM computer system. Because CRM systems are based on Internet technology, the sales reps' data can be sliced and diced faster than we would have imagined possible just a few years ago. Your staff personnel analyze these inputs and build a forecast. The manufacturing, production, and logistics departments then mobilize their efforts and construct building schedules for the products along with delivery plans. Products are then built and shipped, customers are billed and are satisfied, and life is good!

Question: How does this business cycle support your strategic requirement to develop 20 trusted relationships? It doesn't! It assumes those 20 relationships already exist. Something's missing, something big.

If you are an executive, that something missing is you!

You are the missing link in these scenarios. Two executives can make more decisions in an hour than their staffs can make in a year. But no executives are present in this typical business scenario. Those of you who depend on other companies to take the risks of implementing your new products or ideas are the missing links in these opportunities.

Generals don't want to hear inputs from soldiers about how they should be running a war. Similarly, your potential strategic alliance's executives don't want to entertain your sales reps when you're asking them to take a business risk on your new product or service. They want to see their peers from your company; want to know them; want to compare notes and ideas with them; want to decide if partnerships are possible; and want to have peer-level relationships with partnering organizations. They want to develop a sense of trust in you before they move ahead with a business risk.

Consulting firms have several cultural attributes that help them handle these kinds of requirements. They routinely match their partners with their clients' top executives. They match generals with generals, colonels with colonels, strength on strength. They organize and manage themselves in ways that help to build relationships with clients naturally and easily. The following three elements of their business ensure their success in creating and maintaining critical relationships:

1. Organization
2. Process and practices
3. Interpersonal skills

THE PARTNERSHIP PYRAMID
AND RAINMAKERS

Most traditional business executives have risen to the top ranks in their companies through their mastery of a business model that recognizes and promotes employees based on their ability to delegate key responsibilities to other staff members. As owners of their firm and functioning as their firm's generals, consulting partners do delegate certain business decisions and activities to their staff. But this is where consultants break with the military analogy. Contrary to typical business practices—most likely those in your own company—*partners, their firm's generals, do not delegate accountability for creating client relationships to their employees.* They accept that accountability personally and are referred to as *rainmakers* in their firms as a result.

Rainmaker is a term that exists in the lore of Native Americans, referring to the tribe member who was assigned responsibility for creating rain to nourish the crops in the fields, thus feeding all the members of the tribe. Partners in consulting firms accept the designation of rainmaker with a great amount of pride. The less experienced members of their firm aspire to achieve that informal title in their career paths.

Although the most obvious relationship-building capabilities possessed by consulting partners are usually assumed to be their interpersonal skills, the organizational structure illustrated in Figure 3.1—the Pyramid—is equally important to their success, because it enables these relationship-building skills to work effectively. Let's begin by taking a

FIGURE 3.1 *The Pyramid*

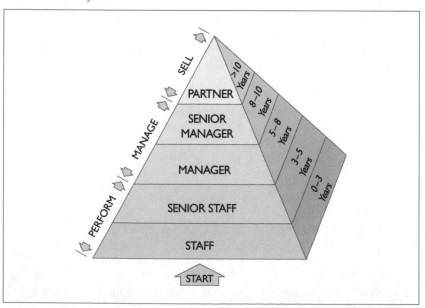

closer look at this unique organizational structure, and then we'll explain and analyze the interpersonal skills of a typical rainmaker in a following chapter.

The view of the Pyramid that we present is intended to be a generalized, simplistic example that allows us to highlight its most important features. Like any organizational scheme, it is more complex than we can show here. (See Figure 3.1.) The five layers depicted in the illustration are basically the same for partnerships in all types of professional firms—audit, legal, architectural, and consulting come to mind here. We haven't covered all of the specific positions that may exist for every layer in the interest of time and space. We'll start at the bottom layer of the Pyramid, where almost every member of the firm starts his or her career. (See "Consulting Firm Competencies" in the appendix for an appreciation of the skills that make the levels of the Pyramid work.)

Staff

Young, eager, highly motivated current college graduates are hired by the firms, whereupon they are placed immediately in junior staff positions. Here their first priority is to be trained in the processes and practices of their firm. A large portion of their initial training is in the classroom, but they are also introduced to real-life client projects through participation on project teams, performing "gofer" tasks at first. It is also at this early stage that these young members of a firm are assigned to one of the firm's areas of specialization. These areas might include such specialties as technologies, software applications, and business applications, some of which may be specific to an industry segment. Some of the technologies include networking infrastructure, client server, and wireless. Software and business applications include salesforce automation, human resources management, supply chain management, and the like.

PricewaterhouseCoopers, the largest global consulting partnership, at one time claimed it had more than 14,000 staff members specialized in a software application package from SAP, AG. Many consulting firms have also instituted a specialty in supply chain management to address the needs of clients who need to streamline their entire cost structure.

Young employees spend three or four years in staff positions, learning their specialty and developing expertise in the firm's processes. Those we've interviewed and worked with contend that the most effective learning takes place on the job as they rotate through many client team assignments. Consider this career development track carefully. Young people are provided on-the-job training by watching how the more senior members of the firm conduct the firm's business. Once a staff member has facilitated and worked with the same processes and practices in several client engagements, usually in a specialized industry segment like banking or manufacturing, then that staff member is able to exhibit genuine business acumen at a very early stage in his or her career. The senior employees of the firm who teach the staffers how to conduct their business are performing a function known as *mentoring*, and mentors reside at all levels of the Pyramid.

In mentoring, the operative thought is to "do what I do, not what I say." Mentoring is a primary responsibility of a rainmaker and is regarded as an extremely important aspect of the care and feeding of the "tribe." Few military generals and colonels would accept this kind of accountability. Remember that many traditional business practices are modeled after our military, not Native American tribes.

Senior Staff

Staffers who prove to be adept at learning and executing processes and practices are moved into more senior roles after a few years. Promotion to senior staff comes with an expectation that senior staffers will now become mentors as they assume team leadership responsibilities. It is not unusual to see fairly large numbers of staff people "wash out" of the program; many find employment easily with client organizations that want to take advantage of the process and application expertise the staffers gained during their short consulting careers.

The great majority of a consulting firm's employees exit at some point during their development, which is a design feature of the Pyramid. Note its shape. You'll see relatively more space at the bottom, with space becoming more and more constricted as you progress toward the top. Practically all partners boast of having started at the staff level, and they are proud to have survived the up-or-out realities as they have risen in the Pyramid.

This up-or-out practice brings two distinct advantages to a consulting firm. First, it allows the firm to continue to refresh its ranks with young people who bring enthusiasm and high aspirations to the firm. Second, and just as important, this practice keeps the cost structure of the performing portion of the Pyramid relatively low. That is, the cost structure is low relative to what it would be if people were kept in low-level positions for longer periods; their salaries and benefits would have to be raised in a fashion similar to the way traditional companies raise salaries for individual contributors of long standing. The only way to be a long-standing employee in a consulting firm is to survive the up-or-out practice, which means the firm's partners feel that survivors have the potential to become partners.

The effectiveness of a consulting firm's staffers is ensured through two factors. One, on-the-job mentoring teaches processes and practices, but it also enables the more senior-level staffers and partners to evaluate the performance and potential of newer recruits. Second, this practice works because the firms have bulletproof, proven engagement processes that can be executed by inexperienced people.

Managers

Those who demonstrate staff and senior-level staff capabilities are constantly being evaluated to determine if they have management potential. In most firms, a high percentage (more than 50 percent) of staffers fail to satisfy a firm's requirements, and many staffers are asked to leave at this point. Those who don't make the cut are still young, and they are readily employable because of the skills they learned in the firm. Many firms actively place these people into their key clients' organizations, where they keep a relationship alive from a distance. We've heard partners from various firms refer to these departed employees as their *alumni*. One global firm we work with conducts a golf outing every June in Atlanta to which they invite hundreds of their alums to play golf with the partners and current managers of the firm.

Think how these alums must help a firm's relationship-building efforts with a key client once the partners have placed them. Further, contrast this practice with the outplacement methods that are probably followed in your own company when you ask someone to leave. Traditional businesses don't merely burn bridges with employees that they release. They blow them to smithereens! This unique outplacement technique is just one of the elements that make consulting practices such formidable relationship builders.

The entire emphasis at the staff levels is on the efficient and effective execution of processes and practices. Staffers are similar to soldiers, the difference being that young consultants learn practical lessons from their colonels and generals. Focus on processes begins to change at the management level. Anyone who has attended a project management class can tell you that project management is about 10 percent methodology and 90 percent interpersonal skills. Manager-level people in a consulting firm are like military captains in being accountable for meeting tactical milestones, or targets, for client projects. But unlike staff members, they are also required to learn how to mentor their project teams. An interesting wrinkle in consulting is that a manager's team also includes client personnel.

A staff member who is promoted to manage must demonstrate a command of the firm's engagement processes and methodologies as well as the ability to be a mentor; a promoted staffer must also be able to leverage the business acumen that has been developed through many client engagements. In most businesses, process-oriented individuals are not expert practitioners of the soft skills required for leadership and team building. Similarly, few of a consulting firm's staff members rise to the top of the Pyramid.

Senior Managers

Senior management positions are filled by those managers who have proven to be candidates for promotion to partner. Managers at this level represent a small handful, perhaps 2 to 5 percent, of entry-level staff. These people may have from 10 to 15 years of experience in the firm, and they now find that the partners are personally mentoring them on a frequent basis. After all, if senior managers are going to have a shot at becoming a partner, mentors want to make absolutely sure these are people that mentors can live with as fellow owners of the firm.

Senior managers are often called *practice leaders* because they assume total responsibility, perhaps global responsibility, for one of a firm's areas of specialization. These specialization areas are called *practices* and are staffed with people from all levels of the Pyramid as appropriate. The size of a practice depends entirely on the amount of business—the number of engagements—that the firm is conducting for that specialty. The PricewaterhouseCoopers SAP practice, referred to earlier, may have several practice leaders spread over many geographical areas and covering various aspects of the practice.

Senior managers are expected to become involved in the communities where they live. Consulting firms are often recognized for the way they give back to the communities that support their business. Let's face it, community involvement, whether in the ballet, the symphony, or a program to help the disadvantaged, is a pretty effective way to meet old and new clients in a meaningful way as well. I noticed during the 1996 Olympics in Atlanta that many of the prominent leadership positions that ensured the successful execution of the games were filled with partners and senior managers from what were known in those days as the Big 5 accounting firms.

Partners

Consulting firms are partnerships. Partners own their firms and are responsible for defining how service plans and client assignments combined with their own past experience, capabilities, and personal interests support the firm's strategies and operational plans. Do you already sense that these people differ from executives who run more traditional companies, perhaps a company like yours? They certainly differ from military generals. Five distinguishing characteristics of partners are described below.

1. **Partners own all of the stock in their respective firms.** Executives in publicly traded companies never approach this level of participation through stock option grants. As owners of their business, partners divide net profits among themselves at the end of each year. They share resources when asked because they are all on the same page at year-end and are therefore more motivated to mutually assure each other's success. They don't spend time competing with each other for higher positions— because there are none. The largest firms may have a titular head— sometimes called the *managing director*—but the opportunities to advance beyond partner are very limited. The point here is that owners act differently than employees.

We have heard many consulting partners express disapproval of the way a lot of corporate salespeople toss around the term *business partner.* Although consultants work diligently to create teaming relationships with their clients, they would never invite a client to become a business partner with them. Those who have experienced business from a partnership perspective feel that inviting a customer to be a partner of any kind is a false claim, because the person issuing the invitation doesn't really mean that he or she wants to share resources and/or split the cost of goods or services. Have you ever invited customers to be business partners only to find them asking you to split your billing 50-50?

2. Partners are mentors. Partners have proven their ability and desire to mentor junior staff members and client personnel during their rise up the Pyramid. They don't prefer to manage from behind a desk because they have to stay involved in the community and in the firm's engagements in order to be rainmakers. Remember, partners have been mentored up the Pyramid over the course of their career, and they are well suited for teaching their processes and practices to younger team members. Every partner exhibits personal responsibility, and a vested interest, in accelerating the technical and professional development of staff members, both to improve the quality of work and increase retention of the best people.

3. Partners are the best executors of their processes and methods. Every partner assumes a responsibility to provide leadership for the firm in the conduct of firm activities. These include recruiting, staff counseling, continuing education, and specific administrative responsibilities. They know the process methodology inside and out because they have never strayed from working on client engagements. They were mentored in these processes, and they have mentored others as well.

4. Partners are visible in the community. To be a leader in the community each partner strives to be recognized as an active and qualified participant in the community. Partners ensure that all business, professional, and civic organizations are aware of the firm's capabilities and professionalism. Directorships, trusteeships, and leadership roles with highly visible business, professional, and community organizations are key elements of a partner's role. Partners are expected to give speeches to local and national business and industry groups and publish articles in leading business magazines. Partners are always looking for opportunities to be of service to community organizations, thus putting their best feet forward to strengthen the firm's reputation and visibility.

5. Partners are rainmakers. They "own" the accountability for creating and managing client relationships. This requires an entrepreneurial state of mind, a highly tailored approach, and a skillful application of resources to achieve desired results. These requirements differentiate partners from most corporate executives more than any other point we could make. Every partner has a special responsibility to develop superior services tailored to the clients he or she serves. Partners focus on their specific contributions to service quality and client satisfaction.

Developing client relationships includes:

- Spending substantial on-the-job time at the client's office
- Identifying ways to improve client services and satisfaction
- Discussing new service opportunities with client executives
- Broadening knowledge of the client's business
- Increasing the number of executive relationships

PERFORM–MANAGE–SELL

Contrasting the Pyramid with traditional business organizational practices should help you understand why consulting and audit firms

B *efore* **Y** *ou* **M** *ove* **O** *n . . .*

Answer the following questions:

1. *How many customer relationships do you manage personally?*

2. *What has been your observation of consulting partners? Where do they work best?*

3. *How effective are you at dealing with your customers' executives?*

4. *Do you consider yourself to be a mentor? If so, how and whom do you mentor today?*

5. *How would you assess your relationship development skills?*

have such good access to your customers' top management as well as to the top echelons of your own company. An approach made by a peer is more difficult to shuffle off to lower-level staff members than an approach made by, let's say, a 25-year-old salesperson. This also might explain why it often becomes an exercise in futility when you try to compete with a consulting firm by selling against their recommendations.

Here's an interesting way to view the career path of a typical consulting partner. Look once again at "the Pyramid" on page 28 and think about the process that takes place over time as people are mentored throughout their career. In their first career step, everyone *performs* on client engagements when they learn to facilitate processes and methods. Performance work is highly valued by clients who pay handsomely to have such work done. Staff members who show the ability to progress in a career are promoted to management positions where they learn to *manage* both projects and people on the job in client engagements. Finally, only the managers who display the right interpersonal characteristics and are believed to be capable of being rainmakers are given the responsibility to *sell.*

Partners accept accountability for selling only after they have accumulated a significant amount of business acumen from hundreds of engagements in specialty areas. That's why your sales reps feel overmatched when you ask them to compete with consulting partners; it's no wonder they feel that way. Compare the training and experience rainmakers have accumulated during a career spent climbing the Pyramid with the sales and product training your sales reps received before assuming quota responsibility. If you are an executive, perhaps it's time to reassess the expectations you have for your salespeople.

An IBM area sales vice president from Dallas was sitting in the audience at one of our sessions a few years ago. When we offered our description of how partnerships conduct the *Perform–Manage–Sell* model, he approached the front of the room, turned our flip chart of the Pyramid upside down, and then returned to his seat. Stunned, I asked him why he did that. Pointing at the upside down chart, he replied:

> *That's us! The first thing we ask new employees in my organization to do when we hire them is to* sell! *We delegate the responsibility of acquiring relationships to these people, and our top managers assume very little accountability for executive relationships. We have no objective way*

to measure the quality of relationships they build. We only measure their quota performance. If they make quota for a few short years, we promote them and let them manage. I can see now why we are so overmatched when we encounter consultants in our accounts.

The IBM executive also admitted that his company was getting a little fat around the middle, meaning that so many people were being promoted into managerial jobs that the organization found it had more people in management than in either strategy or execution. Of course, IBM didn't have a monopoly on that concept either. Many organizations shed much of the fat around their middle as the effects of the economic recession demanded that they balance the needs for greater productivity with the accelerating demands made by Wall Street for increasing earnings per share. Many such companies held "back-to-the-field" programs in which they offered managerial workers—those deemed to be part of the "fat"—a tough choice: "Go to the field and learn how to sell what you do for us to other companies, or leave the company!" Most managers who were affected by these programs had never created or managed key customer relationships, and yet these programs put them in the position of being forced to do just that.

These back-to-the-field programs gave rise to outplacement firms, a group of companies that helped move employees who were declared expendable onto other companies' rosters. The outplaced workers sometimes took jobs as relationship builders. Because they had consistently implemented the "up-or-out" policies, consulting firms seldom had this problem.

Hiring new people to sell, thereby making them the de facto relationship builders, is a common business practice in every industry we've seen. Most companies also try to minimize the amount of time new employees spend in training programs so that the new folks can hit the street as soon as possible after being hired. Contrast that philosophy with the mentoring practices in consulting firms. Which kind of employee can exhibit a greater understanding of his or her company and its products—a well-mentored consulting staff member or a hastily trained corporate sales representative? Maybe this is why corporate sales reps, when hired and hastily trained, are referred to as "gunslingers."

We think this type of poor—or nonexistent—training is the reason so many salespeople move from company to company during their selling career. We've noticed they often position themselves as "sales professionals" to the hiring executives who are looking for people with the proven ability to create relationships. These sales professionals recycle themselves into senior sales, or even sales executive, positions, but few have really ever demonstrated the ability to deal effectively with executives, because they have never been mentored in the art of doing it.

SUMMARY

Consulting partnerships stay within their pyramidal organizational style year in and year out, and they don't look for professional relationship builders on the street. They build their own. The clients of these professional firms know what to expect when a partner, senior manager, or manager shows up on their site to join a project team, because a consultant's job title is a consistent predictor of what that person can be expected to contribute.

MATCH ME IF YOU CAN

MATCHING PEERS

Pyramids are interesting organizations when considered alone, but they do have a more important purpose. The "Matchup" illustration in Figure 4.1 provides the answer to *why* consultants organize this way as a logical follow-up to the question of *how* they organize that we answered in Chapter 3. The illustration in Figure 4.1 depicts the way in which consultants match their organization—Pyramid—with their clients' organization. This peer-to-peer arrangement ensures that the consulting firms' influence is developed at all levels within clients' organizations.

The top priority with any first-strike opportunity is to set up a trusted relationship between rainmaker and client executive; and matching organizational levels—much like matching strength on strength between sports teams—is the first step in this process.

In the final analysis, clients' executives decide how much a rainmaker's quality of service will be allowed to influence their organization. A major consideration in how clients make that decision is the peer-level relationships that rainmakers establish. The checklist on page 41 includes elements that consulting firms use to assess the degree to which they are aligned, or matched up, with each of their clients' organizations.

FIGURE 4.1 *Matchup*

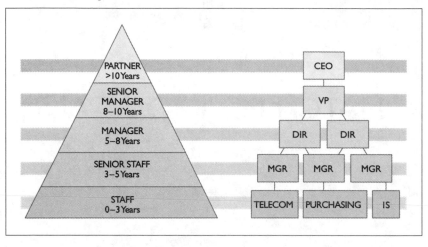

Consider your own company for a moment. Do you match up with your customers and prospects in the manner suggested above, or does your company expect your salespeople to create contacts with customer executives? Do your executives take the lead by contacting customer executives, or do they expect your salespeople to "call at the top"? Delegating this important function to salespeople doesn't work very often. More important, it threatens the valuable relationships that your troops have built with buyers, administrators, and purchasing managers who don't understand why you force your salespeople to go over their heads. Rainmakers ensure that their strategic relationships are built and kept intact at all levels of a customer's organization because they—the rainmakers—are accountable.

Let's look at a real-life situation where a traditional business executive found that his company's culture needed changing to increase his odds for success.

THE CONSULTING SERVICES START-UP

I met with the president of a large electronics distributor and services company in Chicago when I was with Cisco Systems. This gentleman and I had known each other for several years, and he had been a strong supporter of "The Selling Value Tour" we conducted at Cisco for

M a t c h i n g   P e e r s   C h e c k l i s t

Client Executive Awareness

- *How extensive are our executive relationships?*
- *Are we involved with the client's business and operational planning?*
- *Do client executives consult with us regarding critical business issues and decisions?*
- *How extensively are we involved with client executives outside the workplace?*
- *Are client executives fully aware of all of our service capabilities?*

Client Communications

- *How extensive are our relationships beyond top management?*
- *Are we developing relationships beyond the partner level?*
- *Have we held seminars that benefit different levels in a client's organization?*
- *Do we routinely send articles and other items of interest to our key client contacts?*
- *Are we proactively meeting with client contacts to discuss our observations and recommendations?*
- *Do client contacts at different levels request our input on important decisions?*
- *Are we involved with departmental or operational planning?*

Practice Development

- *Do members of a client's management team participate in the client's planning process?*
- *Do cross-functional teams from our firm participate in the client's planning process?*
- *Do client executives recommend us to their business contacts?*

the channel partners. His company had always focused on selling products but found it was giving away consultative services in order to get product orders. A major problem was that the products were always losing their value as they became commodities, so profit margins in the product side of the business kept shrinking. The company quickly realized that profit margins on consultative services were higher than margins on products. Four conclusions it reached after weeks of analysis about the business follow.

1. First—a no-brainer—it didn't make sense to give away the high-margin services business in order to sell more of the low-margin products.
2. Selling services required that the company call at higher levels in its customers' organizations, but its salespeople were unable to remove their focus from their products long enough to focus on the consulting services that were of a higher value to customers than were their products.
3. Realistically, the company couldn't forgo the product business, so it couldn't afford to have product focus diminished.
4. The company's customers didn't perceive its product-oriented salespeople to be trustworthy enough to handle high-value services engagements. Customers had seen them in the FBR-FFF mode and couldn't accept them in a more intimate role.

The president of the company concluded that the only way to keep selling both products and consulting services was to spin off the consulting services business and run it himself. The reason he wanted to see me was to discuss practices that I thought he would need to adopt to be successful in consulting.

I drew the Pyramid on his whiteboard to show how successful consulting practices such as PricewaterhouseCoopers and others involve their total organizations to create a peer-level matchup scheme with their clients. As we just explained, in a matchup like this, all levels of clients' organizations are matched up with the rainmaker's corresponding levels.

The president became noticeably uneasy when he realized that the Pyramid diagram required that *he* personally accept the primary accountability for creating and building his new firm's key relationships. Like most executives, when asked if he wanted his firm to build trusted relationships with key customers, this executive responded, "Hell yes!" But as with most executives in traditional businesses, it had not occurred to him that he would have to accept this job himself. "Relationship building has always been the job of the salesforce," he remarked, "going way back to when I joined this company 20 years ago as a sales trainee." His candid appraisal of that scenario went something like this:

I've got to admit that we weren't very good at it [relationship building]. It always seemed odd to me that management would ask the youngest, least experienced people like us to forge relationships with executives at our customers' sites. But that's just the way it's always been!

I have been president of this company for almost ten years, and I have always prided myself on the amount of time I spend in the field with my sales guys. But no one considers me to be the executive contact with any of our customers! I have always expected the sales guys to do that. I always have felt that we provide adequate training for the sales teams and that they should be able to do that.

So I asked how that was working for him, given that his salespeople couldn't be entrusted to sell high-value services. He answered:

Not worth a damn. None of them have ever been good at calling at the top!

I couldn't help asking him how often he agreed to see sales reps from other companies that asked for his time. He answered:

I don't ever see other companies' sales reps because they waste my time. When they call, I slough them off to someone else.

Well, the irony of what he was saying hit him like a bolt of lightning. He then admitted that he also hadn't been good at making executive calls 20 years ago, when he was a salesman. He also admitted that my suggestion that he should accept personal accountability for contacting customer executives bothered him. He was concerned by how it would look if he, as president, tried to set up an appointment to see another president.

He asked if he might look desperate by taking the initiative to contact the CEOs of his top customers. I asked how often his auditors and other consulting partners that worked for him contacted him, and he said they contacted him frequently. I asked if they appeared desperate or offensive when they called, and his response, alone, could have prompted our writing this book. He said they don't offend him for one reason:

The auditors and consultants only call when they are giving us help.

I kept the conversation going by asking him to explain what he does when he visits customers with his salespeople; he replied:

We go to their accounts, and we call on whomever they can reach. It's usually someone in the purchasing department, perhaps a buyer or one of the user department administrators. I guess your point is that I get myself locked into the low levels of our customers' organizations the same way my reps do, and I therefore create more roadblocks to my ultimate goal of reaching top executives because I also become recognized as a product supplier.

By spending his time this way, the president was also losing the opportunity to mentor his people, a chance to show them how to make executive approaches correctly. *He wasn't leading his sales reps anyplace they couldn't already go!* He had positioned himself as a sales representative.

I realized two issues were on the table here. First, we were battling a cultural element—relationship building had always been delegated to the salesforce. This should be relatively easy to fix given the models and positive examples we could show him. The second issue would be more difficult to address because it involved his ability to develop confidence in himself, personal confidence that he could approach other executives without offending them and without appearing desperate.

This executive was open to learning about how others have overcome similar organizational and personal challenges. He was willing to change his personal accountability when he became convinced that the proposed changes would improve his new company's chances for success. Does any of this feel or sound familiar to you?

HOW TRADITIONAL BUSINESSES CAN REAP RELATIONSHIP-BUILDING BENEFITS

Our intention is not to convert corporate employees and managers into consultants and partners. We also know that it's not possible for you to implement a pyramidal structure in your traditional company. But we do believe that you can become a rainmaker for your business. The principle we have highlighted here, the *peer-level matchup,* can be implemented in a number of creative ways between your executives and their counterparts in your customer accounts.

Executives often express concern about this idea, some of them saying they don't have time to be a rainmaker. But when we ask them what could be more important than promoting trusted relationships with key customers, they'll usually agree with our idea. Peeling back the layers of their concerns reveals deeper, more personal reasons to avoid the responsibility of promoting customer relationships. Some have told us they regard themselves "above performing the sales function." They claim to have invested heavily in their career and feel they're going backward if they yield to our proposal.

In our experience, executives who feel this way can be motivated to change if new ideas are carefully justified. Many executives don't believe they can approach a customer executive with enough credibility to spark a deeper relationship. They display a lack of self-confidence. Many really don't know how to spark a relationship because they've never done it before, including the times when they were sales reps themselves.

We share a personal belief that many executives feel this way because they were never mentored in the ways of relationship building as they grew in their career. Many of them rose through the sales ranks, graduated from FBR-FFF training programs, made their quotas, and were promoted into management in much the same way described by the IBM executive we referred to earlier in this chapter. We deal with the ways we address the interpersonal side of this issue later in the book. For now, let's acknowledge the problem and find a way to deal with its organizational aspect.

PRACTICAL APPROACHES

Let's get practical about your business and look at ways that companies like yours have implemented some rainmaker attributes. The next few pages outline several hybrid Pyramids that have allowed companies to reap the benefits of the peer-level matchup process.

Executive sponsorship programs (ESPs). These programs can be an effective way to link your senior executives to your key and/or strategic accounts. Such programs are intended to facilitate long-term, value-added, executive-to-executive relationships with designated major account customers to optimize the customers' satisfaction and facilitate profitable revenue growth. These are the objectives of an ESP:

- Ensure that key accounts consider you the "supplier of choice" through extensive executive interaction
- Understand customers' key business processes
- Increase the level and breadth of executive relationships
- Articulate your company strategy and value proposition
- Capture and communicate "words of the executive customer"
- Champion the resolution of executive customer issues

In an ESP program, executives are asked to become sponsors for one or more customer situations. The primary role of an executive sponsor is to establish shared value and strategy with customers by strengthening relationships with their senior executives. Responsibilities also include helping to develop account strategy, hosting important customer events, and using personal leverage gained through interaction with peers in customer organizations to open closed doors for key account managers and sales teams.

These are ways the success of executive sponsorship programs can be measured:

- Increased identification of major new business opportunities
- Account participation in joint planning sessions and clear understanding of both organization's strategies
- Effective capture and communication of customers' issues, desires, and needs
- Level and quality of relationships developed and sustained
- Strength of customer loyalty and customers' willingness to partner

Executive briefings. We have seen many relationships sparked through executive briefings. IBM has used these procedures since the 1960s, when sales reps were required to invite their strategic account management teams to attend business, application, or technology briefings that were conducted at IBM's plant sites. The plant sites housed all of IBM's product development expertise as well as the top managers who held profit and loss (P&L) responsibility for the company. IBM expected its sales reps to invite top managers from key accounts and further expected that at least one of the customers' top executives would be invited as well. Because most IBM accounts had no relationship with an IBM executive, an appropriate IBM executive was selected to issue the written invitation. That executive was called the "sponsor" for the specific briefing and would be in attendance to greet the customer management team. IBM even had lodging quarters, called the "Homestead," in New York and California to royally house and feed its guests. Most of the briefings' content was of a technical nature, but customers felt they were being given an inside track to the future. The briefings were rated highly by executives and managers alike.

The problem with this IBM methodology was that there was never any continuing follow-up with the customer executives from the IBM sponsors. So IBM's customer executive contact program consisted of annual briefing events. IBM held such a powerful customer franchise in the market that it didn't have to concern itself with building trusted relationships, a tradition it had to reconsider after the marketplace changed with the introduction of the PC and the Internet.

The Cisco Systems Briefing Model

Cisco Systems has conducted thousands of executive briefings on its San Jose, California, campus, and the Executive Briefing Center (EBC) has been a centerpiece of Cisco's go-to-market strategy since the mid-1990s. In 2001, Cisco hosted more than 6,000 executive briefings in San Jose alone!

Cisco's EBC is in a carefully designed, nicely furnished space that includes several state-of-the-art rooms, kitchen facilities, and temporary office space for visiting executives and managers. The center is located off the main lobby in the main headquarters building, making it easier for Cisco's top executives to make multiple visits during business days when they aren't traveling. Sales managers in the field arrange for the briefings through an online scheduling service. They must provide extensive information about each account's business and must also include background information on all customer personnel who will attend. The sales manager also requests specific Cisco executives and managers to participate based on a customer's particular interest. The briefings are booked on the basis of the availability of the requested Cisco executives.

What makes Cisco's program work so well is that every Cisco executive is measured on his or her performance in briefings as rated by the customers. Executives are ranked monthly on two factors: first, on the number of briefings in which they participated; and second, on the average numeric grade they received through their participation. During 2000, John Chambers, Cisco Systems' CEO, participated in the most briefings, a number approaching 200, which translates to more than one briefing per working day when he was not traveling. Add to that total the hundreds of additional customers Chambers met by simply walking through the EBC and introducing himself, and you can see how a positive leadership example can have an impact on the attitude and performance of an organization.

Needless to say, executives who were deficient in the number of briefings in which they participated or who were at the bottom of the performance ranking, were frustrated every year when bonuses and stock options were given. The spirit and intent of the EBC are well known at Cisco, and every aspiring young manager works very hard to meet and greet as many customers as possible.

Cisco Systems' Executive Sponsorship Program (ESP)

Cisco and other technology companies often refer to their executive sponsorship programs as *major accounts programs*. Cisco assigns account involvement responsibility to each of its vice presidents and directors. Though a program like this will always vary in quality, depending on the relationship-building experience of the designated executives, it provides the structure for implementing the peer-level matchup described earlier.

Participating executives come from every functional area of the company, including manufacturing, finance, human resources, engineering, product marketing, and development. A portion of the measurement of this major accounts program depends on the number of executive briefings and other strategic events that are sponsored by the executive in charge of the account. Cisco executives are expected to conduct at least one on-site visit to their customers' locations each year. Executives who are selected correctly should have many interests in common with the customer they are visiting. A Cisco executive representing manufacturing, for example, will not only present Cisco's state-of-the-art remote contract manufacturing process to the customer during an EBC visit but will also visit the customer's manufacturing sites, where a dialogue usually starts that keeps the individuals in touch with each other.

Many factors ensure the success of Cisco's program, most notable of which is that *executives are measured and paid* on the basis of their personal involvement in these customer-oriented programs. But the programs also work because executives from engineering, finance, and manufacturing, who have never been called on to conduct external relationships before, are asked to deal with peer-level people in customer organizations who have the same interests and problems they do. This program is the closest thing we have ever seen to a Pyramid execution.

A DIFFERENT APPROACH

We received confirmation that traditional companies can implement peer-level matchups when we conducted a seminar for a medium-sized sales organization in Atlanta. This company's industry is irrelevant to our discussion because the principles and outcomes could easily apply to most any organization. We had condensed the material that you are discovering in this book into an executive summary and were attempting to present it in one very full day. Our greatest challenge was to cover all of the cultural and organizational aspects of consulting firms as well as the interpersonal characteristics and behaviors of rainmakers for this audience of over 200 sales, support, and service people.

We had insisted on one main condition before agreeing to do this customized seminar: The top executive team, including the president and his four top managers, would attend along with the rest of the company. The first hour passed smoothly and quickly. But as we hit the point in the discussion where we were explaining *peer-level matchups*, we became aware of a commotion in the back of the room. All of the top executives were leaving! A senior manager at the front table said:

That's the problem around here. We can never get the top guys to engage in any of the relationships with our customers. They just expect us to do it!

We finished the day feeling a great deal of concern. We were fearful that the *peer-level matchup* discussion had embarrassed the top guys, causing them to bolt the room. But we had completely misread the situation. As we were packing up our materials and checking out of the hotel, the chairman-CEO approached us in the lobby and invited us to follow him into another of the hotel conference rooms. We were apprehensive about what was about to happen as we followed our host.

The scene that greeted us was a pleasant surprise! The CEO said:

> *The Pyramid hit all of us like a ton of bricks! To a man we realized that our relationships with the accounts that we consider to be strategic are deficient, and in many cases we don't have a relationship at all. Forget trusted relationships!*

We realized as he talked that he and his team had heard and internalized much of what we had presented. In fact, they were actually beating themselves up because they realized it makes little sense to delegate the responsibility for building relationships with their primary source of revenue—their customer base—to the young sales and support people we were training that day. To top it off, they admitted that over 50 percent of the attendees that day had been with the company less than six months.

Here's the best part of this story. The CEO then pointed to a whiteboard on which the company's strategic accounts were listed, about 50 in total. In a second column titled "Rainmaker," the name of one of the five top executives was written next to each account. The executives had pulled sales reports, selected accounts, matched themselves up with each account based on the information they had about each customer's business, and were discussing what specific measurements they would use on themselves to make peer-level matchup work. That practice has continued in the company ever since that seminar. Over the following 12 months, both their revenue and gross profit percentage increased dramatically.

SUMMARY

Consulting partnerships and the partners who run them approach relationship building as a top priority. The way they organize themselves, referred to in this book as the Pyramid, provides a considerable amount of the impetus behind their success. Traditional businesses can learn valuable lessons from the Pyramid, and they can implement programs and processes in lieu of changing their organizations that will give purpose and direction to their relationship-building efforts.

We outlined some of our ideas for building relationships, including executive sponsorship programs, executive briefings, and major account programs, all of which enable executive peer-level matchups to occur. Whichever program idea you choose, the main point here is that these programs must be driven from the top down; executives must drive them. Any of these programs will fail to meet expectations if they lack top executive ownership.

5

STEP UP TO VALUE

Most of the people we have encoun-
tered in our work agree that consulting and audit partners are effective
relationship builders. Most executives, especially those at the highest levels of management, have a personal relationship with a partner from a
professional firm whom they trust to give them good advice. Many of
these executives don't know about the Pyramid, nor do they understand
that they are involved in peer-level matchups. What they care about is
fairly simple. They want to talk through issues and problems with someone, anyone, who can help them understand their issues and, most important, help resolve their problems.

Our Pyramid provides a structure that matches the most experienced consultants—the rainmakers—with top-level executives. But this
organizational model is only a piece of the pie when we consider what it
takes to become a Trusted Advisor. The other important pieces are the
partners' business acumen and experience, and the interpersonal style
and skills that they possess.

Before we start our discussion about the interpersonal skills that are
found in a Trusted Advisor, let's examine the meaning and importance
of *business acumen*. Executives are not put at ease only because they are
matched up with partners. They feel comfortable with someone whom

they accept as their peer, especially if that person has addressed the same issues that befuddle the executives. The "Value Staircase" shown in Figure 5.1 sheds some light on how business acumen—at least the perception of it—is developed during the face-to-face interactions between rainmaker and client. The fact that rainmakers operate at the executive level, where executives think business acumen is important, leads many clients to equate acumen with trustworthiness.

The staircase metaphor illustrates how business issues separate themselves into three logical groupings. The top region is the domain of the *strategic issues* that relate to *what* a company must do and *why*. Strategic issues deal with broad areas impacting a company, the company's market, or the company's products. These kinds of issues generally deal with priorities that are both current and anticipated, and they drive discussions about acceptable reasons to change policies and practices. Descriptions of strategic issues are usually very qualitative, directional, and often lacking specific time frames for accomplishment. Mission and vision statements usually originate on the top steps of the staircase. People working at this level focus on the *value* of offerings brought to the

FIGURE 5.1 *The Value Staircase*

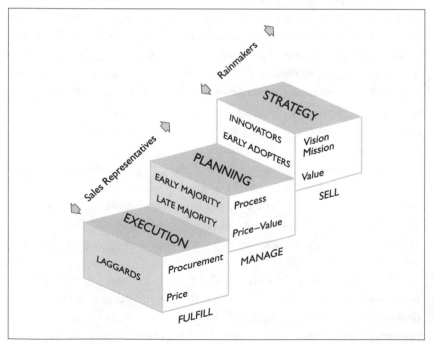

table by alliances, partnerships, and product providers. There is little or no focus at this level on the price of those offerings.

People working in the middle of the staircase deal with *planning and competitive issues* that are more specific than the strategic issues at the top. This is where mission and vision are turned into goals and specific objectives. Whereas the top steps define what must be done and why, the middle region addresses *how* to do what must be done and *when*. Competitive issues, critical to success in the marketplace, are dealt with here. For example, companies are well advised to define whether they will on the basis of price, by being the lowest-cost supplier, compete as a differentiator on features and benefits the competition doesn't have, or walk the difficult and narrow line of a value strategist whereby their products provide significant benefits to consumers.

The recent flurry of restructuring activities—business process reengineering—brings with it a focus on cost reduction and efficiencies that can be achieved. Business process reengineering activity takes place in the middle region of the staircase, where a focus on *value and price* is combined when offerings from external suppliers are being considered.

At the bottom of the staircase you'll find that people focus on *tactical and operational issues,* which are usually driven by either budgetary or competitive factors. For example, a company that differentiates itself on the basis of its customer service puts a lot of tactical focus on the people, skills, organization, systems, and facilities needed to deliver service, as defined by its strategy and operational plans.

The bottom region of the staircase houses tactical schedules and plans, including monthly revenue quotas, financial reports, and product shipping schedules. The plans and programs that are created on these bottom steps drive the daily execution of a business. People working at this level focus almost entirely on the *price* of products and services that are required to satisfy the goals and objectives that have trickled down the staircase to them. It is almost impossible to present a value-based proposal to people who work at this level.

The management teams in most corporations spread themselves over the top two regions of the staircase. Executives and their various top-level teams, similar to generals and colonels, drive their organization's strategy, so they spend much of their time worrying about managing the right vision and mission for their organization. These executives live on the top steps. The executives who actually manage the day-to-day business, majors and captains, work in the middle region. They spend most of their time interpreting and translating their company's vision and mission statements into practical goals and objectives that drive their business results.

Individual contributors, like lieutenants and soldiers, live at the bottom of the stairs and are kept on a short leash when compared with those on the steps above. Budgets tend to be very specific at this level. This is where purchasing departments exist. Purchasing managers make their mark in an organization based on the amount of savings they can generate for the company's coffers. They have specific methodologies to ensure that the products and services procured by the company are bid by multiple supply sources and bid according to acceptable pricing procedures. Remember the new product we wanted to introduce in Chapter 3? Purchasing departments don't have procedures for acquiring new and unproven products, so they usually aren't receptive to looking at them, especially when they can't find two or three other suppliers from whom they can accept bids for the same thing. *Innovation is of much greater interest to people at the top of the staircase.*

Even though we recommend to our clients that they stay away from purchasing managers, we don't intend to demean them or minimize their importance. They actually make most of the decisions to purchase goods and services. The majority of their decisions are based on price, because they assume that the department or individuals who ask them to make procurements have determined the value of the proposed purchase. Rainmakers know that the key to business success is to be in the driver's seat for decisions about products and services, and the driver's seat is on the top of the staircase. That's why rainmakers spend most of their time there. The Pyramid matches up a rainmaker's team members very logically on a client's staircase. Do most traditional businesses pay attention to their customers' Value Staircases in this way? Do you?

Let's review the factors that determine a customer's perception of your product's price and value and see how that perception changes according to the various levels of management on the staircase. As you'll note in this discussion, much of a product's perceived value is based on exactly where it is in its life cycle. But the way in which even the oldest products are packaged is also a primary determinant of their value, and rainmakers are very adept at packaging. The following discussion is especially important to those traditional salesforces that continue to make value-based proposals to people who operate on the bottom steps of their customers' staircases.

PRODUCT LIFE CYCLES

In his blockbuster high-tech marketing book *Crossing the Chasm* (Harper Business, 1991), Geoffrey Moore described what he called "The Technology Adoption Life Cycle." The "Product Life Cycle" illustration in Figure 5.2 depicts this important concept, which applies to most industries. The top line on the curve represents the way sales volume and its corresponding revenue increase to a peak after a product is introduced and how revenues and profits logically decline as the product becomes more mature and its rate of growth slows. You can see that Moore refers to the first users of a product as *innovators*—that is, those people who are willing and able to take a business and personal risk on an idea that is unproven. By the way, innovators drive purchasing managers crazy because the new, highly innovative products they want to purchase have no comparable, competitive offerings in the marketplace on which to seek additional bids!

At the other end of a product's life cycle are the *laggards,* those who adopt a product only after it has proven itself in the marketplace and

FIGURE 5.2 *The Product Life Cycle*

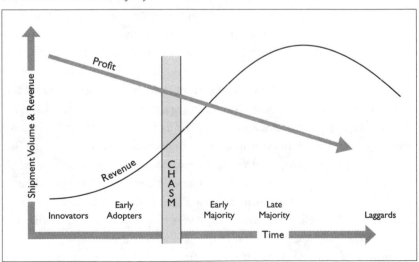

shown that all of the kinks and bugs have been eliminated, making purchasing the product a safe choice. Who are the visionaries in your company? Are they innovators or laggards? It's interesting to be aware of this distinction in your own place of business, but *it is critical to understand the concept of innovators and laggards as it applies to your customers.* Many of the frustrations we have seen exhibited by sales executives have arisen because they fail to understand why it's futile to present their price-based proposals to executives on the top steps of the staircase, who are value-seeking innovators by nature.

Moore explains that a chasm exists between "early adopters" and the "early majority." This chasm is the graveyard where products languish and die if the inventor doesn't understand how to reduce the customer's perception of the risk of using the new product. Silicon Valley and the great dot-com boom produced hundreds of examples of well-funded products that failed the practicality test Moore defines, and they never escaped the chasm. In the diagram you see the early and late "majority," the people who accept the risk to implement a new product once it has built momentum in the marketplace and who become solid references for those who are contemplating purchasing it.

As products enter their life cycle and start the inevitable progression toward the chasm, their *value, defined as the amount of money an early adopter is willing to pay,* is at its highest point, a result primarily of the lack of competitive options available to buyers. This also means that the profit margin available to the new product's supplier is also at its highest point on the cycle when the product is brand-new. That's because a product's age and maturity on its life cycle determines its value and thus affects the potential profitability that can be realized by the supplier.

It should not be a surprise to find that a laggard pays less for an item than an early adopter pays for the same thing because products that reach a high volume of sales attract competition. Higher volumes also give the supplier a cost advantage to produce the product in higher volumes. Silicon Valley marketing managers refer to this high volume–low price and margin phenomenon as *commoditization,* meaning that products eventually become commodities after they have lived in the marketplace for a certain amount of time. Think about VCRs, DVDs, high definition (HD) television, and CD players in this way. These media players reached commodity status very quickly, becoming top-selling items in discount electronics stores within the first year of their existence. As this book goes to print, VCRs have enjoyed an entire life cycle and are being totally replaced by DVDs. Even movie rental stores are converting most of their shelf space to DVDs, which are entering the majority stages.

HD television is still clawing at the left side of the chasm, but its success is almost assured because of the pioneering efforts of its predecessors. Innovators are showing their newest cellular telephone technologies that include full-function cameras built into the phones. Within the first year of this book's initial publication, these innovative televisions and cellular phones will become commodities.

Some commodities are never replaced, and they can enjoy long lives in that status. Wind instruments like trumpets, saxophones, and oboes haven't improved or changed for more than a century, yet children continue to beg their parents to buy them. Because these instruments were commoditized in the marketplace long ago, most parents shop for the best price, knowing there's little value a store can add to the basic student product beyond merely having it in stock. When Mercedes brought their popular S series automobiles to the United Sates in 1999, early adopters paid their local dealers premium prices of 10 to 20 percent above full list price to be the first drivers of these cars. They were willing to pay this premium to reward Mercedes' innovators. Within a year, majority buyers were receiving discounts of 5 to 10 percent off list price for the same cars from the same dealers! There are thousands of examples you have seen in your lifetime where perceived value, price, and available profit margins have decreased with the age of many products you've purchased.

Price and profit available in the marketplace are at their highest point for innovations, just as the risk and perceived value inherent in buying the products are highest for early adopters and early majority buyers. We have added a little more data to Moore's work in what we call the "Marketing Life Cycle." (See Figure 5.3.) This alternate view of Moore's cycle reflects how organizations like yours should sell products and services through their life cycles. At the beginning of a product's life, when value and price are at their highest points and the best prospects for innovation are visionaries, the new product must be *sold*. New products need to be sold because demand for them has not yet developed. Prospective users don't know about their existence and haven't any data to instruct them what a reasonable price would be for these new items.

In order for innovators to *sell* new product ideas, their own organizations must first understand the new product in great detail; understand

FIGURE 5.3 *The Marketing Life Cycle*

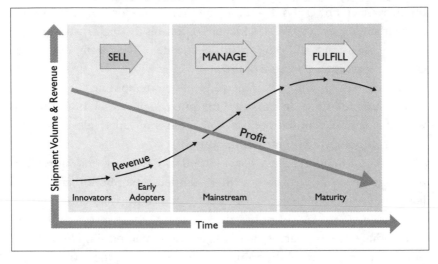

the perceived market need that will drive customers to buy it; and collaborate with initial customers to such a high degree that the product is
pushed into the marketplace.

We have observed that sales professionals have a difficult time selling innovative products. When they do attempt to sell, they need a lot of
help and involvement with customer calls from the new product's innovators, who are typically inventors, engineers, or authors. When we say
sell, we are referring to the first phase of this cycle and don't mean to
imply that salespeople should therefore be entrusted with a new product's successful introduction. Most sales professionals tell us they become stressed out with new product introductions because their first
priority is always to continue making quota by selling what's "on the
wagon!" Rainmakers are sometimes engaged to help a client analyze innovative items, but they don't dedicate significant resources to the
items—that is, building practices around them—until the products have
proven themselves in the marketplace.

Once a product has successfully jumped over the chasm, Geoffrey
Moore insists that the most important activity for the inventor is to "just
ship it!" Moore refers to this somewhat frenetic phase of shipping new
products to the early majority as the "Tornado." This is the time when
the innovator builds market share leadership by getting as many of
the new products shipped in as short a period as possible. We call this

phase of our marketing life cycle *manage*, because the primary value that the selling organization can provide to customers is to manage the deployment of the new product in an orderly, professional manner for its customers.

As new products gain momentum and volume begins to build, sales professionals find they can write orders with a smaller investment of their time. They create referrals from their early success stories about how other majority organizations are using their new product. Advertising begins to have value during this phase, but strong public relations stories and articles are the most effective marketing tools. This is the phase when sales professionals earn their largest commissions and therefore provide their maximum value to their customers and employers.

Purchasing managers become involved at this point to analyze the innovation in the *manage* phase because their own majority buyers, who clearly sit in the middle of the staircase, begin to ask for pricing guidance on the new products as they gain momentum. When this stage is reached, many rainmakers begin to build practices within their organizations to help their clients manage the deployment of the new, rapidly accepted product that is proving its mettle.

Commoditization rears its head when high-volume distributors begin to buy and stock an innovator's products, but the products are no longer "new" at this point. We refer to this phase as *fulfill* because the primary value that can be added at this time is to fulfill the demand for the high-volume orders that have developed in the marketplace. At this point, the innovators feel competitive pressure from other products as distributors negotiate the lowest possible prices for large quantities. This forces the products' creators to use advertising to pull the products through distributors and into the hands of end consumers. The buyers at this point in the cycle are late majority and laggards. Profit margins available to the products' creators are a fraction of what they were at the early adopter stage by this time, and much of the sales function can be handled by telephone sales reps and online ordering systems.

As margins shrink, it becomes difficult for companies to support the typical commission rates that fund most sales compensation plans. Thus, the role of sales professional becomes cloudy with respect to selling commodities. Some companies find ways to bundle support and other services around a commodity, thus regaining some of the profit margin that evaporates over time. Companies also look for value-added channels of distribution that will perform this value bundling for them. Innovators' companies discovered long ago that it isn't practical to continue to pay regular sales commission rates when their available profit margins are reduced because their products have become commodities.

By the time a product reaches the fulfill stage, the perception of its value in the marketplace has dwindled. The only way for the innovator to realize acceptable profit is to increase production volume, reduce price, and reduce selling expense. Margins can be pumped up only through creative packaging, or bundling, of the new commodity with other higher-margin offerings.

Enter the rainmakers! This kind of bundling activity is where they really shine, helping their clients integrate commodity products into the total solution packages they require. To a rainmaker, the profit margin available on a fulfill product is irrelevant. In fact, rainmakers often call your sales reps in at this point to help their clients negotiate low prices from you. The rainmakers make money when they help their clients—your customers—decide to use your product, procure it, integrate it, and train the clients in its use.

ENCORES

We don't suppose that you need a fundamental course in marketing and pricing, so please excuse us if the preceding discussion seemed too basic. But we felt it necessary to review life cycles to set up the next discussion. Thriving companies face a problem that is created by their success. The "Cycle Collision" illustration in Figure 5.4 helps to explain this situation. You can see that the life cycle curve for the innovator's first product is still intact, but a second curve is also present, a curve that begins during the majority phase of the first product's cycle. The second cycle depicts the next product in line for release to the marketplace. The second product—we refer to it as an Encore—must be in its development phase when revenue from the first product is growing to maturity. Ideally, the profits realized from the first product's revenues are the fuel that fires the development engine, allowing a second product, or Encore, to hit the market. A successful, thriving company may well have one new product hitting the chasm during the Tornado phase of its predecessor.

FIGURE 5.4 *The Cycle Collision*

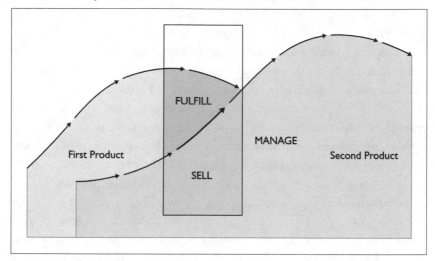

In the world of consumer electronics and high tech, the time horizon for these follow-on product cycles becomes compressed, meaning that the time it takes to get the second product across the chasm is often a fraction of the time it took to get the first product into the majority. We have also observed that Encore products are faster, more reliable, and less expensive than their predecessors. The first cellular phone sold by Pac Bell in 1985 for installation in an automobile carried a retail price of around $3,800. Does anyone remember paying $400 for a VCR? How about the first portable personal computer that was sold by Compaq for more than $10,000?

In 2002, Andy Grove, chairman of Intel Corporation told a staff meeting of Cisco Systems' executives that the life cycle of an Intel microprocessor, the brains of a computer, was less than 11 months. In the 1970s, IBM boasted that the life cycle of its major computers' brains was 7 years. This means that Intel has to have Encore products designed almost at the same time as the predecessors are hitting the chasm!

You may want to assess the impact of this situation on your own company. We believe that the tremendous productivity increases that are driving global economies are creating a dynamic competitiveness from which no industry can escape.

What do these collapsing time frames mean to your salesforce? As you can see in the illustration, *sell* and *fulfill* activities often occur simultaneously. This is a blessing and a curse for any company that has to create a Tornado for a new product while continuing to ensure market share gains and profitability for older products. It's a blessing because the company is proving it can continue to be innovative. The phenomenon reinforces our belief that sales professionals are best utilized during the manage phase of their products' life cycle. It's a curse because few sales reps that we've ever met can split their focus and handle both sell and manage activities with customers. Sales professionals usually default to approaching everything with a manage mentality, which exposes sell opportunities to commoditization more quickly than is necessary.

During the *manage* phase, early majority and late majority buyers need information. They need a sales professional to educate them about the new product or service, and sales reps have to focus on these opportunities without worrying how to contact and sell customer executives on the merits of innovative offerings. Assuming we're right that sales professionals can best focus on *manage* with majorities, then it follows that people other than sales professionals should focus on *sell* and *fulfill* requirements. As we mentioned earlier, channel partners and telemarketing services are effective ways of handling commodities at fulfill time. All of this leaves us with the following important question:

Who should focus on innovators and early adopters at sell time?

The answer in the Pyramid is simple and straightforward. It's the rainmakers, the top executives in their respective firms, who do it. Unfortunately, the answer to our question in traditional companies like yours is not so simple. Traditional businesses keep testing their sales professionals with this function, and they continue to be disappointed.

PRICE AND VALUE IN A PARTNERSHIP

We have just described dynamics that make it a tricky proposition for any company to realize maximum value from each and every product that it produces. Consciously or unconsciously, companies negotiate their way through the chasm, release their products, sell them, support them, put them to rest, and introduce follow-on products. The cycle repeats itself again and again and again! But is there not a learning curve? We continue to see companies spinning their sales professionals into this compression chamber without stopping to consider why it doesn't work well—why the exciting products they believe to be innovative are sold by their salesforce based on pricing and why their innovation becomes commoditized so quickly. Engaging sales professionals in high-value *sell* activity with innovative customer executives seldom works.

What are rainmakers doing while you are seeking early adopters for your new products and bidding your mainstream products to the majorities? They can be found matching themselves up in your customers' organizations, helping your customers' executives define their missions and strategies. Rainmakers operate on the top steps, where they can help with strategy development, a position that inevitably leads them into the more practical arena of business process reengineering.

So What?

The fact that rainmakers spend their time on the top and middle steps in your customers' organizations poses big problems when you want to sell a new product but don't recognize and handle the situation properly. Unless your new product is a simple replacement for a commodity that your customers already know they need, you'll have to compete with rainmakers for your customers' attention and then show them how your product complements the business that is under way. To navigate this condition, you'll need an introduction into the right levels of the management team that is working on these issues. The purchasing managers who buy your mainstream and commodity products will probably not be of help to you in this endeavor, which means you'll have to find an innovative way to see the executives and managers that you need to see.

Assuming that you secure an invitation to meet, your next issue will be deciding whom to send into the opportunity. Your first impulse will probably be to send a sales professional. Trust us on this: Your customer would rather meet with a responsible executive or manager from your engineering or manufacturing department or with a functionary in your development organization when considering a new, innovative product. Doing this effectively demands that whomever you send must adopt the style and demeanor of an innovator and must understand your product from the ground up. In addition, you must invest time and money to learn the requirements that you may be able to meet with your product.

On hearing our point of view on this matter, most companies respond as follows:

- "Our top executives and managers don't have time to spend traveling to customer sites."
- "These same top managers are neither trained nor equipped to discuss customer requirements, and they are beyond handling selling tasks in their career."

Such responses give credence to our assertion that consulting partnerships and traditional business organizations do things in very different ways. When a Pyramid matches rainmakers to the highest-value business activities for clients, it ensures that rainmakers are dealing with their clients' visionaries—the executives who have the most appreciation for innovators. Most corporations don't do that. They wait for rainmakers to put their stamps of approval on their products. When you allow that to happen in your accounts, rainmakers do your *sell* job, and it encourages your customers to beat you up over your pricing.

Think about the staircase and the value versus price dilemma in the context of sending your sales professionals into battle. Lacking a point of entry to the top decision-making levels and facing constant pressure to be more productive in achieving their tactical sales quotas and targets, sales reps usually forfeit their contact activities to the places where they are most comfortable. And those places are on the bottom steps of the staircase where price, not value, is the driving factor for success.

Product companies, caught in this situation, find that their customers are able to strip away any consideration of value for their products because their innovative products are viewed through the lenses of the people who receive the proposals: the purchasing departments. Remember, this is where prices are driven downward. We have seen this problem hit our clients' profits countless times. Sales reps will actually propose new products in bids designed to procure commodities, and they'll do this even when there are no competitive offerings in the marketplace!

SUMMARY

Rainmakers keep themselves focused and involved with the issues and services that have the highest value to their clients. They match up on the top steps of the staircase with their clients' executives and match the rest of their employees with the middle and lower steps. This matching keeps rainmakers focused on the highest value components of their clients' solutions. It also ensures that they keep personal accountability for the development of new relationships.

Traditional businesses like yours have much to learn from this model. To emulate some of these rainmaker concepts, you'll have to free yourselves from the notion that your own top managers and leaders don't have time to visit customers. Your executives and managers can be trained to participate in high-value activities with other executives. We ask: Is it fair to expect a sales rep to carry your story into a customer's top management area where the rep must invest considerable time competing for attention against veteran, highly specialized rainmakers? Or does it make more sense to send your executives and top managers to get that job done?

How can you develop your own rainmakers and mentors? We'll look next at some of the processes and interpersonal skills that form the foundation of the rainmaker's relationship-building prowess. Then you can decide if you and your management team can move upward on the Value Staircase.

6

THE WHEEL OF FORTUNE

Trust opens the door to something far more important than an engagement. Trust opens the door to a relationship.

Rainmakers create relationships through a combination of processes and interpersonal skills. Let's leave traditional selling behind at this point and look closely at the processes and practices that enable rainmakers to create trusted relationships.

Rainmakers become successful throughout their careers by constantly demonstrating a strong reliance on process. This dedication to process is demonstrated and taught to all potential rainmakers beginning on the first day they are employed by their firm. The way rainmakers demonstrate on-the-job processes and practices to their employees is mentoring. This chapter deconstructs the processes that rainmakers use when they focus on doing business with both newly acquired and existing clients. Most of the following information has never before been documented, so you could put it in the category of the fabled "grandmother's meat loaf recipe." It is handed down—one generation at a time—by consulting partners via word of mouth and through on-the-job demonstrations of processes when rainmakers mentor their employees.

THE CREATION CYCLE

The creation cycle—we refer to it as the "Wheel of Fortune"—delineates many of the processes and actions that rainmakers invoke when they create a new, profitable business. The client relationships that are developed by using our model help to improve their fortunes. This intriguing model, illustrated in Figure 6.1, involves seven steps, each of which encompasses many attributes. A wheel is an appropriate metaphor for this model because a rainmaker's goal is to move relationships forward with the kind of momentum that will sustain and keep them moving in a positive direction.

Rainmakers take every client engagement personally because their relationships with clients are conducted on a highly personal basis. Rainmakers treat each engagement as if it is unique, and they do this even when they have seen similar issues with many other clients. A friend who had suffered a heart attack once told me: "Yeah. Lot's of people have had this condition. But this heart attack is *my* heart attack!" Clients want to have their issues treated with that same kind of respect, and that's why packaged solutions seldom wear well with executives in crisis mode.

In each and every engagement, rainmakers are focused on delivering high-quality service that meets the client's needs, is cost effective, and is completed within a reasonable time frame. When a rainmaker conducts an engagement, he or she needs to be as confident as possible that he or she understands what a client wants, although "wants" may not be expressed in an eloquent fashion. Constant contact with a client beginning with step one in this model—prospecting—allows the client to observe the rainmaker's style, competencies, and work ethic. The client's favorable or unfavorable perception is greatly influenced by the level of comfort that evolves during the prospecting process. Demonstrating energy and effort toward understanding the client's wishes, issues, and personal style is therefore a natural part of a rainmaker's activity.

A rainmaker's tactical execution in the model encompasses two elements:

1. Understanding the client's situation thoroughly, including the way the client thinks and how the client approaches issues
2. Using each contact with the client as an opportunity to let the client see how the rainmaker works and thinks

FIGURE 6.1 *The Wheel of Fortune*

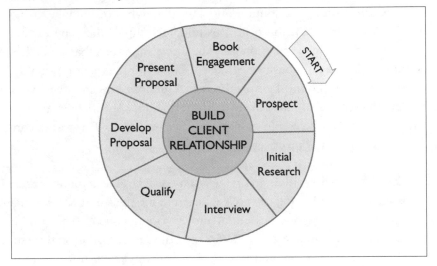

See Appendix B for specific creation cycle tactics for understanding clients and demonstrating service excellence.

Most business leaders, especially those who handle sales, react in a predictable way when they see our graphical illustration for the first time. They remark how dramatically different it is from the sales processes they have learned and have subsequently inculcated into their salespeople through myriad training programs. Recall how rainmakers mentor their people in processes when they lead by example. Most traditional sales leaders train their people by sponsoring seminars and classes run by outside, third-party trainers. *Rainmakers lead by example, whereas corporate executives delegate the same functions to their staffs.* Let's examine the seven steps in the Wheel of Fortune individually to see how rainmakers lead their clients as well as their own people when they are developing relationships.

1. Prospect. We won't spend much time commenting on the first step. Unless yours is a pure retail operation where your customers appear randomly, we believe you know your prospects and have assigned them to territories based on some logical pattern you've developed, such as geographic location, size of operation, or industry specialization. Although some rainmakers are also specialized to serve an industry segment or some other specific business area (manufacturing shop floor, financial systems integration, distribution and logistics, software manufacturing and distribution, etc.), the processes and techniques they employ are generic and can be executed in most business situations that arise. The point here is that most businesses like yours are not looking for new ways to identify prospects for their products and services. You know who your prospects are. You are most likely frustrated about your inability to turn the prospects you have into customers. (See Appendix C for ways consultants identify new prospects.)

2. Initial research. Rainmakers invest a considerable amount of their personal time conducting research to learn as much as they can about a prospective client before they initiate any personal contact. They find it almost impossible to delegate this research function to other staff members because the information that is obtained will shape how the rainmaker will make the initial contact. The rainmaker must *own* this kind of sensitive information and truly understand it to use it properly. Most of a rainmaker's engagements come through references, so the research starts by learning as much as possible about the prospect from the referring party. Before the advent of the World Wide Web, you would find rainmakers browsing through magazine and newspaper articles in business college and public libraries, but the Web has greatly simplified and shortened the research process for rainmakers and students alike. Rainmakers want to know the following about prospective clients before attempting a personal contact:

- *Personal profile of their peer-level executive,* a summarized biography. How long has the executive been there? What functions has the executive performed? What has been the person's track record? Where did the executive come from? What was his or her educational background? Community involvement? Hobbies? Positions taken on issues that have appeared in print? Predisposition to using outside resources when solving business issues?
- *What is the customer's primary business?* How is the company positioned in its industry? Is its market share increasing or decreasing? Does it compete on value or price? Who are its primary competitors? What are the major issues confronting the prospect's

industry, for example, labor, government regulation, foreign competition, financial performance, stock price, history, and so on?

- *How is the company organized?* By divisions? Subsidiaries? Is it an integrator or manufacturer? Is the organization chart hierarchical or flat?
- *What is the company's culture?* Stiff and rigid? Loose? Anarchic? What is its dress code? Its philosophy on granting stock options to employees? Are all employees shareholders? Does the company have a reputation as a good place to work?
- *What's the prospect's financial condition?* Is the trend an increase or decrease in gross margins? Is the prospect known for "hitting" the numbers? (Check Appendix D for the Client Profile form.)

3. Interview. *Pay strict attention to this step because it spells out one of the biggest differences between sales reps and rainmakers.* The initial contact that a rainmaker makes with an executive in a prospect's organization is not referred to as a "sales call." Rainmakers refer to this initial meeting as an "interview," even though their strategy is to sell services to the client. Understanding the answers to the research questions enables rainmakers to prepare for, and conduct, interviews effectively—that is, in a way that allows a rainmaker to ask penetrating, well-thought-out questions designed to prompt prospective clients to answer with candor. The depth of a client's answers is a function of the depth of the questions being asked. Pause for a moment and think about the differences that are implied between the two terms *interviews* and *sales calls.* Even though we haven't yet provided a detailed description of an interview, we know you have participated in many sales calls as either a buyer or a seller. Which of these two types of meetings would seem to have more appeal to you based on even the little bit of discussion we've had so far? We spend a lot of time later explaining the structure of an interview, showing how rainmakers use research data to prepare for and conduct every meeting they have with their clients. Interviews are the most effective vehicles rainmakers have found to turn opportunities into billable engagements. Sales calls, on the other hand, are monologues wherein sales reps present their products. Interviews are filled with questions, questions promote dialogue, and dialogue promotes mutual understanding, which is one of the foundation blocks of trust. (See the Client Interview Checklist in Appendix D.)

4. Qualify. Some customer opportunities that rainmakers uncover in their interviews are naturally more inviting than others. They take great care in selecting the right opportunities because every engagement they accept means committing their firm's precious resources. Rainmakers meet with each other frequently to review all of the opportunities in front of them, and the selection process is fairly democratic. Opportunities are usually selected or rejected based on the following kinds of criteria:

- The *urgency* of the situation according to the prospect is a telling indication to rainmakers. Rainmakers don't assign priorities they hope a client feels for a situation, but there must be a real sense of urgency demonstrated by the prospect's executive(s).
- The *clarity* of the problem or issue is very important, and rainmakers use a number of tools to help themselves and their clients reach clear definitions of problems before they commit resources to chase after opportunities that aren't clearly expressed.
- There must be evidence that a client's *decision makers are committed* to finding a solution to the issue(s). This is usually not a qualification issue because rainmakers develop these opportunities with a prospective client's peer-level executives. Contrast this with opportunities that may exist for months in the sales forecast of a traditional business, where sales reps make forecasts with no executive decision-maker contact. Rainmakers are honest with their colleagues about a competitor's presence in a situation. A competitive situation usually means that someone else got there first and developed the definition of the issue. Competition can be an indicator that margins will be lower.
- If the client situation is immersed in corporate *politics,* rainmakers try to understand the politics and how the politics will affect them if they pursue the deal. Competition and politics are two of the top reasons why rainmakers decline some opportunities.
- Rainmakers are very careful when they define opportunities, because they have to be *realistic about the resources* that will be required to complete each engagement. They don't want to underestimate what it will take to do the job, nor do they want to commit too many resources. Either type of mistake can produce personnel and financial losses.

- Finally, each opportunity that is considered by a group of partners, or rainmakers, is analyzed to understand its *relationship to the firm's objectives*. Firms tend to stick with what they do best, and they want every client engagement to produce a positive reference they can use later on when they seek other engagements. Trying to do things that are "one-offs" is usually discouraged for this reason.

We'll digress here to show you an important tool you can use immediately that allows a closer inspection of some of your current opportunities. The "Opportunity Assessment Matrix," shown in Figure 6.2, is one example of the kind of qualification tool that rainmakers use to assess business opportunities. We have also helped our corporate clients use this tool effectively to analyze their potential development investments. It works especially well for service providers.

The vertical axis is labeled "Possesses Current Resources," and the horizontal axis is labeled "Odds to Repeat." These are two critical conditions that drive rainmakers' decisions to accept or reject engagements. The vertical axis rates the extent to which a proposed business opportunity will utilize the resources that are already on board. The horizontal axis rates the degree to which this activity might be replicated in future engagements. A high rating here means that working on an activity like

FIGURE 6.2 *The Opportunity Assessment Matrix*

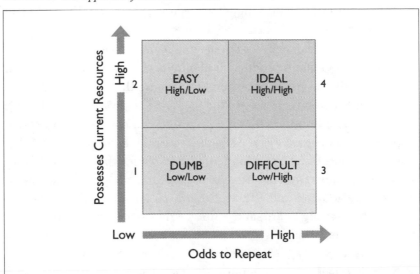

this today is likely to bring greater rewards in the future as resources and experience evolve.

Box 1 *(low/low)* shows that neither of our critical conditions is present. We can't use our current resources and we'll not repeat the same activities in the future. Low/low opportunities are unique opportunities that may present themselves only once or twice and will never be strategic; the tactical implications of accepting them will require development of or hiring special resources that could be better used on opportunities that are more strategic. Box 1 is therefore labeled "Dumb." Low/low activities should only be attempted when a company can obtain the required resources easily. A friend of mine in Minnesota had a favorite saying: "You can fix a lot of things, but you can't fix dumb!" A successful company in the 1990s may have decided to manufacture VCRs to jump on a hot trend. In so doing, it may have acquired people and resources only to hit the wall when the DVD boom hit, and the company didn't have the experience or resources to move to that next important product area.

Box 2 *(high/low)* includes tactical opportunities, and the firm possesses the necessary resources. The bad news: The odds are high that this activity has a short life expectancy in the marketplace. We label these opportunities "Easy" because it's easy to engage in activities for which you have the resources and experience. Commoditized solutions belong in this box. There is little short-term risk in taking these opportunities, but it's advisable to also be working on strategic activities because profit margin always erodes in easy activities.

Box 3 *(low/high)* includes opportunities that intrigue strategists, especially marketing and product development managers. They represent future growth and profit opportunities because they are backed by evidence that demand is growing in the market. The problem here is a lack of the requisite resources for accomplishment. This mismatch between opportunity and resources is difficult to overcome, so we label this box "Difficult." Successful growth-oriented companies drive most of their strategic decisions from this box. An organization that drives itself in this way is always looking to the future, always has an encore product or service on the drawing board, and is not overly fascinated with its own history or past performances.

Finally, Box 4 *(high/high)* denotes the sweet spot for most organizations. It delineates growth opportunities for which the resources are on board. You can probably see the logic for labeling this box "Ideal." A service company that provides products to a specific industry segment or customer type may have invested in a segment when it was difficult to do but later discovers that its products can also be easily adapted to other industries and customers. For example, microchips that used to be sold exclusively to computer manufacturers are now implemented in automobiles, aircraft, heavy machinery, and home appliances. As we go to press, there is a lot of discussion about the promise that the X-ray technologies used in mammograms can also be employed to diagnose heart disease. This is an example of an ideal opportunity for manufacturers of X-ray systems.

Ideal opportunities represent the best potential, whereas difficult opportunities represent strategic potential as well as the biggest need for investment. Done with the right amount of planning, pursuing today's difficult opportunities will create tomorrow's ideal pursuits. There's a message here for traditional companies that thrive in the Easy box. If they plan to stay there, they must continually find innovative ways to repackage, reposition, and promote their products.

The Yamaha Band Instrument Company is a great example of a company that is clearly defined by the Easy box. Brass, woodwind, string, and percussion instruments haven't changed for decades, so Yamaha has pointed its investment strategy at the traditional channels of distribution for band instruments. The market is somewhat stable and actually shrunk when the baby boom slowed and the number of kids available to enroll in school band programs dwindled in the 1990s. Striving for innovative ways of marketing their commodity products, Yamaha began conducting a series of executive briefings in the company's factory in Grand Rapids, Michigan. Music store owners and their management teams are invited to attend these briefings, which are run by Yamaha's top executives. Attendees provide inputs to Yamaha about everything from instrument leasing programs to custom horn designs. Not only are these briefings a creative way to approach *Easy*, but they have led to the formation of a pyramid structure that allows Yamaha executives to stay involved with the customer executives they meet in the briefings. Yamaha's former general manager, Michael Bennett, believes these briefings have not only helped Yamaha cement relationships with its important dealers, but they have also helped Yamaha produce better packaged offerings as a direct result of the input the company received from its valued customers in the sessions. "These new repackaged offerings for our standard products included discounts to the dealers for ordering early, incentives for staying with ordered quantities, and better new features incorporated into some of the instruments," says Bennett. He continues, "We learned the importance of pushing the envelope in packaging our products better by doing one simple thing: listening to our customers."

Rainmakers in consulting firms qualify opportunities with an eye to the ideal. This focus helps professional firms become specialized in an area (by executing the same thing many times) and also improves their focus on building their reputations. Ideal opportunities enable them to mentor new people in the firms' specialties with the knowledge that the new people will have plenty of work ahead of them. When Pricewater-houseCoopers (Price Waterhouse at the time) decided to build an Enterprise Resource Planning (ERP) systems practice based on German company SAP's ERP systems technology, they were rolling the dice by forcing themselves to move from all of the easy practices that had supported them for years into a difficult area. How about the giant bet IBM made by moving from its dominant hardware market position into services? (IBM has acquired all of PricewaterhouseCoopers' consulting practice during the course of writing this book.) The greatest contributor to General Electric Corporation's profits isn't its brand-name manufacturing divisions like appliances, aircraft engines, and lighting products. GE Financial Services is this bellwether's primary profit contributor.

Dumb opportunities can cause profit and growth problems for a rainmaker's firm the same way any traditional business will experience problems by ignoring the future. Occasionally, rainmakers will take a dumb assignment if they have people sitting on the bench and not involved in any strategic activities. The danger is that once resources are committed, they are not available for more strategic projects.

What is dumb for one firm may be difficult or even ideal for another, and consulting firms often refer opportunities to other firms that possess different specialties and resources. This allows the referring firm to develop a relationship with a client by ensuring that the client's needs are well served, albeit by a different firm.

5, 6, and 7. Develop proposal, present proposal, and book engagement. Rainmakers develop most of their proposals on a real-time basis with heavy involvement from their clients. Proposals are therefore customized, not full of boilerplate information. Rainmakers treat a proposal as a critical element of the sales and marketing process and follow basic guidelines to make proposal preparation simple and effective. Rainmakers often use an *engagement letter*, also referred to as a *letter of understanding*. Although this approach is not lengthy or formal, it still establishes engagement expectations in the following ways:

- Defining the engagement parameters
- Summarizing the problems to be solved
- Describing the results to be achieved
- Establishing the time schedule
- Defining client participation
- Stating the fees and expenses

In some cases, a more formal proposal is necessary. As a general guideline, formal proposals contain the following sections:

- Outline of the existing situation—mutual understanding stated in the language of the client
- Nature and scope of services to be provided—areas covered and not covered; approach to the project; where the work will be conducted
- Benefits and results to be obtained—bottom line impact
- Time period for the assignment—elapsed time and project phases
- Fee structure and billing arrangement—fixed fees along with out-of-pocket expenses
- Other considerations—staffing; physical facilities required; special services and supplies; role of client personnel
- References—similar projects for similar organizations

Effective proposals focus on client needs and problems in a crisp, consistent writing style. Graphics and other polishing techniques are important.

Some of our clients through the years have prided themselves on the quantity of boilerplate information they keep in their databases. We've seen this practice backfire numerous times for two main reasons:

1. Too much information is often printed in proposals prepared by sales reps, resulting in customers not having enough time to read

them. This frustrates many customer managers who, in turn, hire consultants to help them read and analyze what appears to be a complex mountain of data. This gives rainmakers the inside track to a trusted relationship.

2. In addition to the issue of information overload, sales reps often don't proofread the boilerplate they include in proposals because they lack the time to do it. So customers wind up looking at out-of-date pricing and product specifications. Worse, boilerplate often contains remnants of proposals to other customers, often including the names of those other companies and confidential references to personnel and business issues. Boilerplate has been heralded as an important productivity tool, but we've seen it damage as many sales results as it's helped.

We'll close this chapter with a short story that illustrates how interviewing customers can prevent problems as well as provide a stepping-stone to a relationship. We know that your company can lift these ideas, unlike some we have presented, and use them exactly the way rainmakers use them. Look within the following story for areas where some of a rainmaker's processes, like interviewing, might work for you. Look also for mistakes that were made that you may be exposed to in your business today. Though this specific situation happened years ago, we still see this kind of behavior exhibited by many of our clients today.

Oscar Mayer Hot Dogs

IBM has always grappled with the concept of the Pyramid, as we noted in our description of its executive briefing program. Many years ago IBM conducted another program, one they called "Intensive Account Planning," into which several high-potential, young managers were promoted as facilitators. Their job was to lead account sales teams through a rigid exercise, usually lasting two or three weeks, to help the account teams develop strategic data-processing plans for 100 of IBM's biggest and most strategic accounts. The sessions were conducted off-site in hotels so that none of the IBMers would be distracted by their normal routines. The program had its merits, but it also had some warts.

When IBM promoted me to a managerial position in Madison, Wisconsin, the home of Oscar Mayer, Inc., I was introduced to my staff in a hotel suite, because they were participating in one of the planning sessions for the Oscar Mayer account. The facilitator flew in from Chicago, and we had about ten of our account team reps and systems engineers in attendance. Also present were some staff people from IBM's distribution and process industry support staffs.

No Oscar Mayer (hereafter Oscar) employees were present; the process excluded customer personnel because the purpose was to determine how much "stuff" we could sell to Oscar. No one at the meeting, including myself, had ever met with a top executive at Oscar. Finally, nobody else from IBM, including the local executive who had been in place for over 20 years, had met with any of Oscar's executives either.

One of the stated goals of the program was to use strategic planning as a lever to put account teams in front of customers' executives, so the first order of business in the planning sessions was to define the top business issue that Oscar's top managers were facing. The facilitator was pretty good at drawing out ideas, and all of us participated freely in the discussion. It didn't matter that some of us had little or no experience in the meat-processing industry. We worked on the top-issue question for more than a week, for more than eight hours every day, and we finally declared victory late one night. One of the visiting staff people had educated the team about the risks inherent in the commodity markets, and pork bellies were extremely volatile at that time. I guess we were comforted by the fact that we'd all grown up eating hot dogs and pork chops because we all jumped into this new information with great vigor!

With the kind of wisdom that could only be generated in a complete vacuum, we decided that Oscar's biggest issue was that Oscar Mayer couldn't control the price of hogs. There were high-fives all around the room. We *were* Oscar Mayer hot dogs! After this high point, the rest of the session was easy.

We spent the next week and a half developing descriptions of what we thought Oscar should buy from us. The account team really shined here, because we were talking about products, and products hit right in their sweet spot. I do remember suggesting to the team that this data processing equipment plan didn't seem to flow naturally from the price-of-hogs discussion. No matter! We did our job, and then a top-ranking IBM executive in Chicago called the president of Oscar Mayer, a gentleman by the name of Bill Schaffer, and scheduled an appointment for us to present our planning results to Oscar's executive team. I was excited about the opportunity to meet the top guys at our biggest account in Madison.

Three more weeks of intensive work followed the planning session as we created our presentation. We had overhead foil acetate slides professionally prepared and printed. We made up copies of the presentation for each one of Oscar's top executives in Moroccan leather binders. We were ready!

We were escorted into Oscar's boardroom when we arrived for our two-hour appointment. Every top executive at that company arrived too. After several minutes of social chatter and coffee, Schaffer invited us to get started. In keeping with our practices, the main sales rep assigned to the account was designated as the primary presenter. He gave a short historical sketch of IBM, introduced all ten of us that were present, and then launched into our presentation. He did a nice job detailing the process that had prompted this meeting, and then he did it! He told the executives that we had wrestled for days over their issues, and up on the projection screen in huge block letters were the words OSCAR MAYER CAN'T CONTROL THE PRICE OF HOGS!

The executives were speechless. The tension in the air was unbearable. When Schaffer asked which one of us was in charge, I raised my hand. He asked me if any of his people had participated in the meeting, and I said, "No!" He then asked me how many overhead acetates we intended to present, and I think I said, "About one hundred." He then advised us to go back to the drawing board, and he terminated the meeting! We all felt as though we had been processed through Oscar's sausage machine!

The only thing I remember after that moment, in addition to being thoroughly embarrassed, is that Schaffer asked me to walk back toward his office with him. He stopped in the hallway, turned and looked me squarely in the eye, and said, "Tom, if you want to know what our issues are, *why don't you just ask us?*"

The Oscar Mayer presentation taught us many valuable lessons. The structure of that program correctly assumed that executives sometimes engage in a positive way if you discuss their issues with them. But you have to be sure that you have identified the right issues for that idea to work. The presentation would probably have run longer had we based our conclusions on solid research. Many facts should have been obtained from interviews with the top executives at Oscar.

The most significant element missing in our relationship with Oscar Mayer was a peer-level matchup. If the IBM branch office in Madison had adopted at least some of the Pyramid concepts, the local sales executive would at the very least have had a conversational relationship with some of Oscar's executives. Responsibility for the Oscar Mayer account had been delegated to many different sales reps through the years, the local management had thrived on Oscar's business, and no top-level manager had found it necessary to create a personal relationship with the company's executives. We had sold millions of dollars worth of equipment to that company over the years, but this situation proved we didn't have a relationship with the company outside of the data processing and purchasing departments.

SUMMARY

Rainmaking assumes that every encounter with a prospect or client brings with it an opportunity to create or enhance a budding relationship. Rainmakers show genuine interest in their clients when they conduct well-researched interviews. They stick to their knitting by employing a rigid qualification process, and they involve clients in customizing proposals for their engagements. At each step of the way, the Wheel of Fortune allows rainmakers to demonstrate their sincere interest in a client. It is the rainmaker's dual focus on the client and the client's issues that fosters trust. The opportunity to start the Wheel of Fortune spinning always exists, even with customers you have known for decades. It's never too late to start.

INTERPERSONAL ATTRIBUTES AND SKILLS

7

THE BIG THREE

We don't pretend that rainmakers are godlike. That's not the point. They have faults, and they wrestle with business issues just like the rest of us. But they have a more focused approach to relationship building than you'll find in most businesses, and their cultures support that approach.

It is impossible to think about rainmakers without considering relationships. Relationships are the lifeblood of a consulting partnership, and rainmakers are the primary instigators of their client relationships. So far we have tried to show how rainmakers are assisted in their relationship building by their organizational methodologies and their cultural adoption of effective, proven processes. Rainmakers find most of their new client opportunities through referrals. They are introduced to new clients by their older clients, who are willing to recommend them because of the high regard in which they hold them. These introductions generally occur at the executive level because that's where rainmakers spend most of their time.

In the following pages we reveal and explain the critical factors for success that drive and sustain rainmakers. You'll find that these factors are transferable to professional partnerships of all types—consulting, legal, auditing, engineering, and the like. We've picked the three most important of these factors for an expanded discussion. The top three factors for ensuring success are:

1. Reputation
2. Relationships
3. Communication style

REPUTATION

Rainmakers are conscious of the importance of referrals, and most will tell you they set goals to ensure their developing each and every client into a satisfied reference. *Reputation* is therefore critical to a rainmaker's success. Reputations are built one engagement at a time and rainmakers who have excellent reputations find that acceptance by new clients comes fairly easy at the first introduction.

Credibility is the main element in a reputation that best explains why new clients engage so easily with rainmakers. Executives wouldn't refer rainmakers to other executives if the rainmakers didn't possess high degrees of credibility where they had worked in the past. If I hear great things about you and know that your credibility is high with others, I might hire you because your credibility with your past associates has sparked an excellent reputation. But that doesn't mean I inherently trust you as well. Trusting you is entirely another matter. We'll discuss the differences between trust and credibility later.

RELATIONSHIPS

Although rainmakers' reputations are the enablers that bring them together with new clients, it's the *relationships* they are able to create with their clients that keep them engaged together. *If credibility is the foundation of a reputation,* trust *is the magic ingredient that differentiates an acquaintance from a* relationship. Most of us accept someone's credibility if we trust that someone, but we don't automatically trust people because they have great reputations. Trust develops over time through multiple performances and contacts for which there are no standard timetables. It takes as long as it takes and sometimes doesn't develop at all. Trust is a very personal thing that largely depends on a combination of perceptions and real data.

To test this theory, think about your own relationships. Earlier in the book we asked you to think about what it takes for someone to earn your trust. Did you answer the question at that time? Can you answer it now? Whom do you trust and why? Do you believe that trust is developed differently in personal relationships than in business? Do trustworthy behaviors look different within the four walls of a company than they appear in a personal, social setting? We don't think there's any difference, and we'll make that case when we explore interpersonal characteristics of rainmakers in the chapters that follow.

Most traditional businesses that sell products don't consider the purpose of their association with customers to be engagements. An *engagement* implies something of longer duration than winning an order for products; and we assume most of our readers' companies fall into this category. We've noticed an increasing number of companies trying to reduce the amount of time they spend on-site with customers in the interest of increasing productivity. Many of these companies strive to replace human touch in customers' offices with online, Web-based communications systems previously discussed. Rainmakers have taken advantage of this situation by engaging with these customers to advise them about buying highly productive companies' products. It's the rainmakers who have earned the role of trusted advisor in those cases.

Rainmakers will control these kinds of relationships as long as product-based companies maintain a short-term focus on their productivity rather than focusing on opportunities to engage for the long term. We believe that your company can participate in these long-term relationships if you're willing to revisit the customer focus you may have lost during the Internet boom.

Evolution of a Trusted Relationship

Trust and *credibility* are not interchangeable terms; they mean different things. The "Influence Model" in Figure 7.1 puts credibility and trust in proper perspective. The first encounter that a rainmaker has with a new client occurs via a referral by a satisfied client. The rainmaker's reputation is the driving force in this type of business transaction, and the rainmaker trades heavily on his or her reputed expertise. The new client

FIGURE 7.1 *The Influence Model*

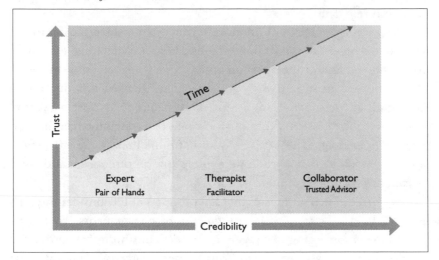

is willing to give the rainmaker the benefit of the doubt on most things at first, because the rainmaker's credibility is high, if only by virtue of another satisfied client's recommendation.

As illustrated, rainmakers are initially perceived by their clients to be another "pair of hands" to accomplish a specific task, such as facilitating a diagnostic session to define a root problem or helping to research an issue. Their reputation carries them in the door initially, after which they have to prove their worth by delivering on their promise of satisfaction. They start their Wheel of Fortune spinning when they execute their interview process, but they can't develop a sense of trust in this early stage. Trust begins to evolve during the initial stages of an engagement, but it doesn't fully develop until the rainmaker has proven that he or she will deliver the results that were promised to the client.

When rainmakers introduce diagnostic processes that will help their clients define clients' business issues, they are able to demonstrate their expertise at the same time. This demonstration brings with it an obvious double focus, partly on a client's issues and, ultimately, on the client's nonbusiness, human side. By mentoring their clients in these diagnostic meetings, rainmakers prove themselves to be concerned, caring business partners, appearing almost as "therapists." Think what actual therapists do: They ask questions and then ask more questions. Their goal is to help their patients reach conclusions on their own, thus allowing patients to retain ownership of their problems and the eventual solution. To rainmakers, every meeting looks like an interview, regardless of its purpose. They resemble therapists in this regard, and they never stop asking questions. (We'll take a closer look at a model for facilitating diagnostic meetings in our chapter on problem solving.)

A major benefit rainmakers realize when they facilitate diagnostic meetings is the evolution of special feelings that bond them with their team members. They all work together toward a common purpose. Trust evolves quickly on these teams as all of the members begin to rely on each other for ideas and inputs. Trust really takes off when teams experience positive results. Check out the way sports stars talk about trust in their teamwork. Kobe Bryant of the Los Angeles Lakers attributes his willingness to take a lot of shots to one fact: He trusts Shaquille O'Neal to always be positioned around the basket to grab the rebound if he misses a shot. Doubles players in tennis say they trust their partners to be in position when they take a chance on a difficult shot. Ryder Cup golfers are willing to take bold chances because they trust that their teammates will pick them up if they lose in their own matches. Members of a rainmaker's engagement team learn they can trust each other when their diagnostic, problem-solving activities begin to bear fruit. As mentors of the client teams, rainmakers also share in the trust that evolves.

The Ultimate Goal: Collaboration

As a result of being mentored, team members develop a high degree of confidence in their own abilities to define and resolve problems. They find they are able to be facilitators themselves of the processes without the need for the rainmaker's constant supervision. When team members get to this point, clients enthusiastically share the initiative and accountability for solving problems. They understand the importance of the rainmaker's mentoring in this context.

At this point, clients' relationships with their mentors become collaborative, meaning they learn to work interdependently with them, sharing both successes and failures. This puts a rainmaker squarely on the client's team where trust evolves naturally. Interdependency and collaboration in one part of a client's operation will often open the door to other areas and opportunities within the company. And rainmakers often find that these new areas welcome them with open arms based on the credibility and trust they have built.

Remember when we explained that a wheel is the perfect metaphor for a rainmaker's engagements because the goal is always getting relationships moving forward with enough momentum to sustain them. *Credibility gives the initial push, and trust provides the staying power.* And it is this combination of trust and credibility that gives rainmakers *The Relationship Advantage*. Relationships don't just happen without purpose and focus. The most precious business relationships to a rainmaker are collaborative and interdependent.

The evolution from "pair of hands" to "therapist" and finally to "collaborator" illustrates the track on which rainmakers evolve into Trusted Advisors to their clients. Does this make sense to you, and can you see why it's so difficult for a traditional sales rep to create this kind of relationship? It takes time, experience, and a reputation for being able to do it.

Sam Barcus has experienced the evolution to Trusted Advisor status with many companies through the years. Listen as Sam relates just one of those experiences.

T h e   I n f l u e n c e   M o d e l   i n   A c t i o n

One of my best personal examples of the evolution from "pair of hands" to "therapist" and finally to "collaborator" is with a former client of ours who had just taken on the position of senior VP of sales for a technology integrator. The company had missed its numbers for the prior 14 quarters, so you can imagine the weight on his shoulders as he stepped into his new role and responsibilities. On engaging with his new employer, we invested quite a bit of time understanding the basics of his business, organization, market, and customers. We functioned as a pair of hands as we conducted a basic, diagnostic survey of the management team, sales, engineering, and customer service. Using the results of the survey, we looked at ways to boost morale with a companywide stock options program.

Our transition to therapist came when we were engaged to identify the real issues and problems that were present in the sales department, which eventually led to the company instituting a major training program on consultative selling. This culminated in our being asked to conduct comprehensive consultative sales training at the company's national sales meeting, after which we were asked to provide real-time, on-the-job coaching for their sales managers. By asking enough penetrating questions and listening to the answers—much as therapists would do—we were able to understand the company's present and future vision. We then collaborated with our client on another project in which we identified and solved the "big" issues we uncovered in our interviews. This evolution moved us into the role of collaborators. Toward the end of the assignment our client paid us the ultimate compliment when he told us that he and his team considered us "both friends and mentors."

The Good News

The kinds of trusted relationships that Sam refers to are not out of your reach. You don't have an executive matchup process in place and your investors and board members are probably asking you to increase productivity by adopting current e-commerce technologies. You're probably wondering how you can reverse decades of traditional sales behavior at the same time you are implementing Internet-based systems. There's got to be some good news hidden among these issues.

Here it is! You already enjoy high credibility with the customers that currently use, and are satisfied with, your products, which means your reputation is intact, albeit your greatest fans are the users of your products, not the executives in those companies. Rather than start anew, your opportunity is to figure out how to move your customer executives' perception of your involvement with them from being a "pair of hands" to a "therapist." You'll find that customers who think you are credible will give you a shot if you'll take it.

The Influence Model discussion serves as a perfect segue to our third critical success factor: communication style.

COMMUNICATION STYLE

During our discussion of the Wheel of Fortune in the last chapter, we briefly mentioned the differences between sales calls and interviews. Sales calls usually involve monologues by sales reps that might be equated to the first ten minutes of *The Tonight Show* on television. During the monologue segment, the host speaks and hopes he's entertaining enough to grab the audience's attention. Even the most experienced TV hosts find they can't be assured of delivering a winning monologue every time. Sales training courses also attach a high degree of importance to grabbing the customer's attention in the first 30 seconds of a call, so conventional sales methods therefore include a structured monologue segment as the introduction to a sales call. The message in these monologues is invariably about products, services, or solutions.

We said that interviews eliminate the monologue issue because their purpose is to start a dialogue. Rather than grabbing the prospect's attention by presenting thoughts or ideas, *rainmakers gain clients' attention by asking questions.*

Rainmakers are confident that their questions will grab their clients' attention because the questions they ask are based on the research they conducted about the prospect (step two on the Wheel of Fortune). Few of us can resist the temptation to answer questions about ourselves and this is especially true if the questions hit on things that absorb us, like our interests, beliefs, activities, or issues. We'll cover a lot of material about how to construct and ask questions later when we explain the Compass in Chapter 11.

Monologues and dialogues are two vastly different communication styles, and they help to delineate the basic behavioral differences that sales reps and rainmakers exhibit during their first contact with a customer. The frequently taught, high-payback communication skill that typifies the behavior most sales reps employ during their monologues is *presentation*. Most dictionaries offer several definitions of this word, which can be summarized as follows:

Presentation: *The act of offering for acceptance or approval; a performance, as of a drama; a formal introduction*

The millions of training classes, seminars, and books covering this topic that are bought and given to sales reps during their sales training programs focus heavily on enhancing presentation skills. A presentation is a monologue in which a sales rep talks and the customer listens and evaluates what is presented.

Many of your customers don't have to waste their time in sales presentations about your commodity products. They can learn what they need to know from your catalog or by tapping into your Web site. In traditional selling, a presentation about the features and benefits of a product is the first order of business unless the prospect is unfamiliar with the vendor, in which case the vendor will open his monologue with a presentation about his company, his company's financial results, customer references, and so on. Remember the story about the IBM rep's presentation to the large bank in Canada? That situation captures perfectly the way a presentation too often becomes the default discussion technique that sales reps use in traditional sales calls.

Sales reps and executives who are considered to be masters of this craft take presentations to a new level when they create what many sales managers refer to as an "elevator pitch." In this kind of monologue, a complete story about a company and its products must be told so succinctly that the entire story can be told in the time it takes to ride up ten stories in an elevator. Needless to say, elevator pitches don't encourage interaction or dialogue! I'll never forget these words that I heard a Dale Carnegie teacher speak in a class:

People judge you more by the quality of the questions you ask than by the amount of information you know.

These words meant much more to me after I became a rainmaker. Rainmakers use presentations too, but we use them much later in our process. Understanding that no solution should be presented unless a problem has first been defined, and also knowing that monologues don't help clients define problems, rainmakers focus on creating a dialogue as their first order of business. They don't have to present information about their firms because they have been referred in most cases. In cases where the prospective client requests information, they may send introductory information about their firm in the letter that confirms their appointment.

The Alternative Communication Style

Instead of trying to open their meetings with presentations, rainmakers rely on a communication skill called "facilitation." Checking our Webster's dictionary, we find *facilitate* and *facilitation* defined as follows:

Facilitate: *To make easier; help bring about*
Facilitation: *The act of facilitating*

Rainmakers use facilitation for a variety of purposes. Here are a few:

- Guiding discussions
- Giving instructions
- Questioning and listening
- Paraphrasing
- Giving and receiving feedback
- Building consensus

Appendix D spells out these points in greater detail. Facilitation is an enabling skill. It enables dialogue, and dialogue enables a relationship to start moving forward. Rainmakers use their facilitation skills to help their clients discover pertinent solutions for their issues. They know their clients will feel enabled when they can think and talk freely.

Facilitation and Interviews

Nowhere is facilitation more important than in an interview, and interviewing is not found solely in the domain of rainmakers. Television celebrity Larry King is known for being more than just another host because he possesses exceptional interviewing skills. In a current television commercial for his nightly show on CNN, King says, "It's not about me; it's about the people on the other side of the microphone."

In other words, King doesn't see his job as delivering monologues. He creates an easygoing interview atmosphere where he demonstrates a high level of comfort with the situation and the interviewee. His open demeanor coupled with his knowledge of his guests' subject material gained through personal research enable King's guests to feel at ease.

A wonderful reference about interviewing can be found in the August 2, 2001, edition of *Rolling Stone* magazine. Jonathan Cott conducts a wonderful interview with Studs Terkel, the noted American author, in which Cott calls Terkel "the greatest interviewer of modern times," citing the "documentary masterpieces" he created. Cott recalls that John Kenneth Galbraith, a famous author in his own right, has called Terkel "a national treasure" because of the way Terkel has depicted so many ordinary people in his writings.

When Cott asks Terkel to describe the qualities that define a great interviewer, Terkel answers by quoting the Spanish poet Antonio Machado. See if Machado's quotation doesn't summarize most of what we'll write about facilitation in this book:

> *To engage in a dialog, first ask a question, then listen!*

Terkel puts interviewing in a context that describes effective rainmakers when he describes his craft as follows:

> *What do I compare myself to? A gold prospector. I hear about a person and put in my stake. Digging and digging and digging. And we start the interview. Then I dig up all this ore—a ton of ore—until I've got these thirty pages, single-spaced. Well, you can't use all that. Now you've got to do the sifting. I sift. I've got this handful of gold dust in my hands. And I edit at the key moment. Then I'm a brain surgeon. You've got to do it elegantly so you save what is the truth. You highlight it like a play. The words are the words of a person, though you can alter their sequence. And now I've got my gold dust—and so now you become the director of a play. You're three things: gold prospector, brain surgeon, director of a play.*

What a great description! Terkel's words very naturally fit our purpose of describing interviewing in a context that everyone can grasp. "Prospecting" can be equated to research; "brain surgery" with diagnosis; "sifting" with qualifying; and "play Director" with facilitator.

Is the distinction between facilitation and presentation becoming clear? A presenter stands up, seeks the lights and camera, reaches for the microphone, needs to perform, and seeks approval for his or her actions. A facilitator may try to remain seated, avoids the lights and cameras, offers the microphone to the audience, enables the audience to perform, and gives approval rather than seeking it.

Traditional business leaders often feel that conducting an interview means giving up control of the conversation, something they have been taught never to do. If you perceive that we are telling you to give up conversational control in your interviews, consider this: There is no higher degree of control possible than being in the position of directing questions at others and giving them approval for their responses. Conducting executive interviews demands that rainmakers ask questions first and then deal with the answers they receive. It is ironic that leaders who fear giving up conversational control may be giving away opportunities to exhibit their leadership effectiveness.

Few business books reference interviewing and facilitation to any meaningful extent. We found the following kernels in *Enlightened Leadership* by Ed Oakley and Doug Krug (Stone Tree Publishing, 1992):

> *By asking questions leaders help people discover for themselves what is important for them in doing what is necessary. This discovery process improves their self-confidence and self-esteem, empowering them in the process. Concurrently, they take ownership of the solution, because they have participated in developing it.*

None of the tools available to an interviewer for getting information are as powerful, yet simple, as the ability to ask questions. Effective questioning begins with knowing *what* questions to ask. A practitioner of effective questioning should first develop a framework of the issue being considered and then have in mind a flexible plan for what questions to ask. Knowing *how* to ask questions is equally important. Effective interviewers possess the ability to ask questions that are simultaneously open-ended, searching, probing, and encouraging—and they avoid asking questions that allow only a yes or no response. We'll devote most of Chapter 10 to the subject of questioning and effective questions—how to construct them and ask them.

In *Tough-Minded Leadership* (American Management Association–AMACOM, 1989), author Joe D. Batten appears to refer to rainmakers when he tells business leaders that their first responsibility is to "clarify the purpose and direction of their organization." Then, to do this, he encourages business leaders to go to step two, which he says is simply:

ASK / LISTEN / HEAR

Sometimes we dwell so much on how and why to ask questions that we forget another important part of questioning: listening. Batten distinguishes listening from hearing. To paraphrase, he says that listening enables you to perceive the words being used; hearing enables you to understand what the words mean.

Listening requires more than sitting immobile and nodding in order to be effective. It involves active participation, meaning that listeners become actively involved with the responses they receive to the questions asked. Participation includes verbal responses of encouragement, paraphrasing, and reflecting feelings and nonverbal involvement, such as good eye contact and encouraging gestures.

Understanding these differences enables business leaders to retool their vocabularies to exhibit what Batten calls an "Interrogative Leadership Style." He further points out that insecure managers find it difficult or impossible to do this because they have spent their careers subconsciously building defensive statements and approaches in their business dialogues. Many of the techniques and processes that are taught in sales training classes would fall into the category of "building defensive statements." Rainmakers use this interrogative style seamlessly when they are mentoring their own people as well as client personnel, because interrogative attributes are the foundation of effective facilitation.

ADDITIONAL SUCCESS FACTORS

Although reputation, relationships, and communication style are the three most critical factors, the following factors also drive a rainmaker's success.

Problem-solving skills and tools. Rainmakers are problem solvers. That's what distinguishes them from other business types, especially salespeople. As we'll demonstrate later, facilitation is a rainmaker's primary problem-solving skill. Facilitation is what rainmakers do; how they do it involves tools and techniques that are part of their culture. (We examine one such problem-solving tool later in our discussion of executive interviews.)

Methodologies, tools, and techniques that rainmakers introduce to clients through facilitation enable clients to define and solve problems. Their methodologies are so well documented that a firm's new recruits can be mentored in their use rather quickly during recruits' first client engagements. Mentoring by rainmakers ensures that the recruits will come up to speed quickly. The fact that they can start billing for their time early in their career keeps their firms' cost structures competitive. The mentoring of skills, along with well-documented tools and techniques, ensures that this can happen.

Negotiation. When they are closing a deal, rainmakers negotiate engagements with a mind-set different from that found in traditional businesses. Just like FBR and FFF, salespeople have been taught to negotiate win-win agreements. The basis of this concept is that a compromise can always be reached that satisfies both parties. Rainmakers want to avoid haggling by trying to compromise, so they often employ a lose-win strategy that allows the client to win at the same time the rainmakers appear to lose something. (We'll show how this works in our subsequent discussion, "Singles versus Home Runs." Rainmakers who want to get the Wheel of Fortune spinning don't allow themselves to get bogged down by a negotiated compromise. They plan on staying around for a long time and know that money issues will equalize over time.

Team building. Rainmakers grow their own peoples' skills through on-the-job mentoring. But mentoring doesn't stop there. Rainmakers also mentor their clients' employees during engagements because *clients are the most important part of an engagement team.* Rainmaking operates on the condition that clients should always retain ownership of their problems. Because rainmakers don't want to assume ownership of a client's issues, it follows they facilitate issues in such a way that clients are credited with creating solutions to their problems. In fact, successful rainmakers won't accept engagements unless their clients participate, because they don't want to be solely responsible for the solution.

This ownership philosophy explains why rainmakers are so eager to share their methodologies and tools with client personnel. Rainmakers applaud their clients for the work they do and seldom do they seek applause in return. Think about that for a moment. Do your sales reps enable your customers to solve their problems, or are your reps expected to present solutions that solve problems for your customers? Do you ever applaud your customers' efforts and teamwork, or do you only reward your reps when they make a sale? To summarize this brief discussion, rainmakers thrive on their ability to mentor their clients' personnel as well as their own. This kind of team building is critical to their success.

Practice development. This refers to the methods and processes that rainmakers use to develop engagements with new and current clients. The Wheel of Fortune is one such process, and each element we have discussed in this chapter implies that rainmakers are growing their businesses by executing the elements while concurrently mentoring their own people. Rainmakers are always following their business development processes, whether working with current clients or engaging with new ones.

SUMMARY

We hope this discussion about a rainmaker's critical success factors has answered many of the questions you had about how and why rainmaker culture differs from your own. Reputation, relationships, and communication style shape the way rainmakers behave. Following are some of the ways rainmakers are perceived by their clients to have differentiated themselves based on the critical success factors:

1. *Rainmakers are proactive about obtaining business for their firm and never delegate this important job to their newest employees,* which is one of the most significant ideas we present and also represents the biggest challenge to traditional business leaders who want to emulate rainmaker attributes in their own business.
2. Rainmakers invest their own time conducting research to understand the issues that are impeding their clients' businesses.
3. Given the option to ask questions or present ideas, rainmakers always ask questions.
4. Rainmakers define problems before they consider solutions.
5. Rainmakers approach every situation believing that each can be turned into a long-term relationship.
6. Getting an engagement rolling forward is more important to a rainmaker than winning half of the spoils in a win-win negotiation.
7. Rainmakers operate with a strong sense of team, and their teams include people from their client organizations.

8

THE BEST-KEPT SECRET

Dale Carnegie wrote his best-seller *How to Win Friends and Influence People* in 1936, and his principles live today in the behavior of effective rainmakers. The following two quotations from his book summarize very well the interpersonal attributes that most often characterize rainmakers:

> *You can make more friends in two months by becoming interested in other people than you can in two years by trying to get other people interested in you.*

> *A show of interest, as with every other principle of human relations, must be sincere. It must pay off not only for the person showing the interest, but also for the person receiving the attention. It's a two-way street where both parties benefit.*

A RAINMAKER'S SECRET

Reading Carnegie's words helps all of us understand the major interpersonal characteristic that cuts through all of the facts and data we can present about rainmakers. We'll turn to The PAR Group, an Atlanta-based training firm specializing in a course called "Leadership and Team-work" to help us define this characteristic.

PAR conducted an interesting survey in which it asked sales represen-tatives from many different industries to answer the following question:

> *As a sales professional, you know that you should call on the decision*
> *makers in your key accounts. Why don't you do that?*

The responses PAR received shed new light on the commonly held belief that reps stay away from calling at the top because they fear rejec-tion. Rather than outright rejection, the respondents' fear was that de-cision makers wouldn't think they were interesting! They were scared to death that top executives wouldn't be interested in what they had to say or present.

Trained presenters can select the best material, practice a presenta-tion in front of a mirror, practice with a friend, put on their best business attire, and make a presentation in the most articulate manner. Even with all of this, they are still handicapped by fear because audiences may not find their presentations interesting! What a fascinating revelation! The fear of subjecting oneself to that particular kind of disapproval might cause any of us to quake in our boots. Sales reps often tell us, "There's no way that the executives in my accounts want to hear anything I have to say." Down deep in their hearts they are afraid that the executives won't think they are interest*ing.*

Many of us have experienced these feelings in our personal lives. For example, one of the most difficult tasks in coaching Little League players in the art of hitting a baseball is teaching them to create and hold what's called a "positive swing thought" as they prepare to hit. This re-quires the player to be thinking about *How* he is going to connect with the ball as opposed to wondering *If* he can hit it. One youngster I coached always leaned backwards when the ball was pitched to him. When I asked him why he didn't stand in the box and swing at the pitches, he told me, "If I swing the bat, the ball will hit my hands!"

That little guy didn't have a positive swing thought! League rules wouldn't allow him to skip his turn in the team rotation at the plate, but he could chicken out once he was actually batting.

Sales reps express their versions of swing thoughts differently, but the end result is the same.

Taking PAR's lead, we have asked thousands of salespeople who have attended our seminars the following question:

Do you believe with total confidence that the top executive in your most important account will think that you are interesting when you make your next presentation?

Even the most self-assured seminar participants are not willing to respond with a rousing yes to that question. On the other hand, almost 100 percent raise their hands in the affirmative when we ask this next question:

The next time you meet with top executives in your most important account, could you be interested in them?

There it is! That is a successful rainmaker's greatest secret: IF YOU GET NOTHING ELSE OUT OF THIS BOOK, BE INTEREST*ED*.

A GREAT TREASURE

I vividly remember the first time I heard Jim Georges, CEO of The PAR Group, present the important distinction between being *interesting* and *interested*. Wow! The hair stood up on my neck. In fact, it still does each time I relate this secret to someone who hasn't heard it before—like right now! I have flashbacks to countless difficult situations since my encounter with Jim. I conclude, perhaps too harshly, that I had been insulting people for years, and they had put up with me because I portrayed all of the characteristics that were expected in a sales guy. In all my years of selling, I had never had time to be *interested* in my customers because I was too busy selling! How about you?

This distinction between being *interesting* and being *interested* and the behaviors they engender are at opposite ends of the interpersonal universe. We have found that this is the greatest treasure you will discover as you seek to understand how to create trusted relationships in business or in your personal life. Rainmakers are able to contact and meet with the clients they want to pursue largely because of their pyramid organizations and processes. But contacts and meetings don't build trust. *Trust is built through interpersonal actions.*

Think about your own experiences. Can you think of an incident where someone that you didn't know came on too strong to you? Maybe they tried to present something that wasn't appropriate to your needs or your mental state of mind at the time, or maybe you just didn't want to think about the presenter's subject at that time. Did a telemarketing rep get too personal by calling you by your first name? Was a salesperson a little too helpful? Maybe a waiter tried to sell you a bottle of wine before asking about your taste or what you planned to order from the menu? Does it bother you if a stranger assumes something about you without taking the time to get to know you first?

Let's go back to the Montreal bank example again. How do you think the president of that bank felt when the sales team presented a lot of information to him about the banking industry along with a healthy dose of specific information about his own bank? Keep in mind that the bank president is more of an expert on those topics than the sales team could ever be. That team was trying to knock the president's socks off by showing him how much they knew. They probably thought their presentation would earn them a peer-level position with the president, so they tried to be interest*ing*. The reality is that the banking presentation represented the way things are done by most traditional businesses.

How about Oscar Mayer and the price of hogs? For all we know, our conclusion was correct, but if so, the Oscar Mayer executives already knew it, and we insulted their intelligence. If it weren't true, we assumed something that we needn't have assumed. Remember, Schaffer said he would have told us what their issues were had we *asked*. In retrospect, he probably thought we weren't interested enough to ask.

Seasoned sales reps, sales managers, and executives often find the prospect of changing the focus of their customer conversations—from telling to asking—to be full of insurmountable problems. The concept of asking instead of telling—being interested instead of interesting— just doesn't compute. Many sales executives express the concern that all of this is too "fluffy" for them, sounding to them like wasted time that can be put to better use writing orders and installing products. So they would rather stay in their groove and continue to tell stories than ask questions. Often the "telling" becomes patronizing, as in the Montreal bank example. If you're guilty of doing this to your customers, think about this: *Telling people something they already know to prove that you know it too is as intellectually dishonest as telling people what they want to hear.*

Trust can't exist where manipulation rules.

We hope you are tracking along with us in this discussion and have thought about how rainmakers would have handled the real-life situations we've presented. Their research activities would have included asking customer managers a lot of questions during interviews. The customers would have felt that the rainmakers were interested in them. Why? Because we all ask questions when we are interested in something. Asking questions in lieu of giving presentations brings the same information to the table; the difference is that customers can be given credit for knowing and contributing information found through questioning. You can stay in the background, away from the floodlights and microphones when you ask questions.

Can you usually tell if someone's interest in you is genuine? Would you feel comfortable with a stranger asking you questions about your area of expertise, or would you rather sit and listen while that stranger tells you all that she knows about your subject? Which approach would inspire your trust?

A senior sales rep in a seminar once raised his hand and said, "I guess this process requires that we learn how to fake being interested." He was comparing being interested in an interview with asking formula-based questions that are included in sales training methodologies. This reminds us of our earlier discussion about empathy when we cautioned against saying "I know how you feel" to someone who is expressing a problem or concern. People are all made differently, but most people can tell a fake from the real thing. *It is virtually impossible to fake sincere interest in another person without being caught.*

When we try to be interesting, we put all of the pressure in the situation on ourselves. It calls for the spotlight, the microphone, and the cameras to be pointed at us. Trying to be interesting is like giving a performance, and it puts the audience in the position of being compelled to construct a critical review of the performance. Sales reps know that executives aren't apt to be interested in product presentations, so they often add complexity and dramatic content to pique the interest of the customer. Neither reps nor executive hosts are comfortable in these performances. No wonder salespeople and other junior-level staffers "wimp out" of making executive contacts!

Conversely, being interested in someone else turns things 180 degrees and makes the other person the focal point of the conversation—the most distinguishable characteristic of rainmakers.

SUMMARY

Dale Carnegie had it right. We say, "Ask, don't tell. Facilitate, don't present. Be interest*ed*." What more can we say?

Among the tribes of northern Natal in South Africa, the most common greeting, equivalent to "Hello" in English, is the expression *Sawu bona,* which literally means, "I see you." If you are a member of the tribe, you might reply by saying *Sikhona,* "I am here." The order of exchange is important: Until you see me I do not exist. It's as if when you see me, you bring me into existence. This meaning, implicit in the language, is part of the spirit of *ubuntu,* a frame of mind prevalent among native people in Africa below the Sahara. The word *ubuntu* stems from the folk saying *Umuntu mgumuntu nagabant,* which, from Zulu, literally translates as: "A person is a person because of other people." If you grow up with this perspective, your identity is based on the fact that you are seen—that the people around you respect and acknowledge you as a person. Being interested aspires to the mutual respect and openness that is embedded in the spirit of *ubuntu.* By being interest*ed* rather than interest*ing*, a rainmaker invokes the client's potential by a willingness to see the essence of the client.

9

A MODEL ENGAGEMENT

Traditional businesses can learn to leverage the credibility they already have with their customers, if they are willing to change their approach to customer relationships.

Interest*ed* behavior is the foundation of effective interviews that rainmakers conduct when they are trying to understand a client—and why the client is having a problem. We established that prominent interviewers like Larry King ask questions to obtain answers that they hope will capture the attention of their viewers. Conducting interviews in business situations is no more complicated than a television interview. Business interviews just sound more difficult to accomplish because they represent such a major departure from the cultural norms that you have always adhered to in your traditional business.

Your traditional cultural norms are nowhere more apparent than in selling your products. We know that executives participate in a game with their suppliers' salespeople in traditional business culture every day. We have taken the liberty of making up the following scenario, so please—use your imagination. The game goes something like this:

1. A sales rep is invited to present some product information to a customer executive.
2. Anticipating a presentation, the customer prepares by donning a "filter" designed to separate the presenter's content from his selling process.
3. The customer watches and listens carefully, allowing his filter to flush out any extraneous noise.
4. The customer grades the presentation and the presenter. If the customer ever held a sales position, he will mentally critique the presenter's techniques and compare them to the techniques he learned when he was in sales. (Remember, many executives begin their career in sales!)
5. The customer buys or doesn't buy based on criteria he had set days or weeks prior to the presentation!

This is a little tongue in cheek, but there's a ring of truth to it and may explain why so many companies have decided that Internet-based marketing and order-entry tools are acceptable alternatives to direct sales coverage. Sales reps are often so far out of the loop in the development of their customers' needs that they can only wait for the customers to put requirements out to bid. Once they accept the bid specifications, they can simply mail their proposal to the customer. This is especially true when they fulfill commodity orders for customers that don't need prodding to buy.

RAINMAKER BUSINESS MODEL

Rainmakers avoid responding to bids in most cases, making occasional exceptions for government work. They help their clients create bids, but they try never to answer them. Their processes allow rainmakers to position themselves at the forefront of their clients' problem-solving needs. The processes and actions that help clients understand their issues clearly—that is, diagnose their needs—enable rainmakers to position themselves in this way, and diagnostic activities provide rainmakers with the opportunity to demonstrate their value.

The "Engagement Model" illustration in Figure 9.1 provides a macro view of how business evolves for rainmakers as they engage with clients

FIGURE 9.1 *The Engagement Model*

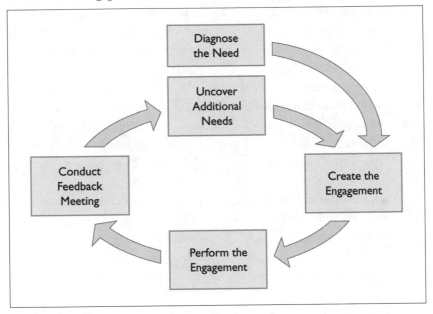

to perform on projects. It provides many clues about how rainmakers turn diagnostic facilitation into long-term relationships. We wrote previously how rainmakers facilitate problem solving during every step in a client relationship, activities that are most important in the initial stages of an engagement.

Step One: Diagnosis

Imagine telling your doctor that your chest feels tight, only to receive this hasty response: "You obviously need a heart transplant!" What's missing in this scenario is a solid diagnosis, defined by *The American Heritage Dictionary* (New College ed.) as follows:

Diagnosis: *The act or process of identifying or determining the nature of a disease through examination*

Most of us would not respond positively to a prescribed surgery that was not based on a thorough diagnosis, would we? Our discomfort would increase or diminish depending on the part of our body in question, and the heart would rank right there at the top.

Business leaders feel the same way when solutions are prescribed to them for curing important issues that haven't been clearly defined through rigid examination or diagnosis. A troubled CEO we'd been working with for a few weeks once remarked to me, "Tom, you're the first guy to ask me questions about our product integration problems. Everybody else who comes through my door tells me what *they* think I need to do, but none of them have taken the time to understand what *I* think should be done. I'm suspicious of people who know the answer before they hear the issue."

I was a corporate executive at Cisco Systems at that time and was developing a Pyramid for our Worldwide Channels organization. Our customer needed us to rectify a touchy situation. Our salespeople had stuffed quantities of our products into this customer's inventory by discounting the products so heavily that the customer couldn't refuse the offer.

We had made a strategic mistake by prescribing lower prices. We could have offered to facilitate a diagnostic session for defining how we could help this customer address his real need: adeptness in integrating our products into his customers' networks. The result was that the customer purchased more products than were required at a time when his real need was advice and assistance to help him move the inventory he had in stock. If the problems behind the integration problems noted above had been carefully diagnosed and if a plan to resolve them was in place, this customer would likely have ordered the same quantities from us, and *he would probably have paid a higher price!*

Diagnosing an issue starts the Engagement Model process rolling, and all other activities flow logically from that act. Failure to participate in diagnosis can lead to unhappy customers or, worse yet, customers who contact rainmakers to do the diagnosis. Rather than offering valuable help to our customer, *we were bidding when we should have been selling.*

Like most process models in rainmaking that create forward momentum, the Engagement Model is also a circular process. The following examination of this model explains how relationships are built through continuous involvement, not through executing bid responses. We have spent many pages developing the idea that rainmakers develop forward momentum with their clients with every action and encounter.

Figure 9.1 shows how that forward momentum is created. Let's consider the steps one at a time:

1. **Diagnose the need.** Driven by their belief that no solutions can be developed until problems are defined, rainmakers use their considerable facilitation skills to define issues and problems as soon as they meet with their clients. This is relatively easy for rainmakers to do because referrals occur with people who need help and often don't know what kind of help they need. Traditional sales reps, and even sales executives, could participate in diagnostic activities as well, but they seem comfortable letting rainmakers do it.

I once asked an Atlanta-based senior partner in one of the premier consulting firms if he was worried about losing business to the traditional companies that were investing millions of dollars in training programs designed to help their sales reps become more "consultative." He told me that he didn't see this as a problem so long as the sales reps continued to carry quotas because "as long as they are measured on product sales, they will never be willing to take the time to diagnose their customers' needs. They'll wait until we have developed bid specifications that spell out which of their products their customers need to buy. They'll continue to act this way because it's the best way for them to increase their productivity!"

Diagnosing the client's need is the pivotal step in the process that makes everything else work. *No diagnosis? No dialogue! No dialogue? No engagement!*

2. **Create the engagement.** Rainmakers write short, specific engagement letters that are similar to the Executive Overview sections in sales proposals. The big difference, as we noted earlier, is that these letters are not sales pitches and aren't filled with boilerplate information. Often, the initial engagement is agreed to and started with an oral agreement; customer executives are frequently considered the worst offenders of their own purchasing policies! Rainmakers approach client executives on a peer-level, captain-to-captain basis where small teams can be committed to diagnostic activities without a formal contract. Engagement letters are often sent as a summary of the oral agreements made between the two executives. Following a diagnostic activity with an engagement letter assures rainmakers they are creating engagements, not responding to bids.

3. Perform the engagement. We have mentioned the importance of credibility and reputation, factors based on a client's perception of the rainmaker's performance. Successful rainmakers do what they say they'll do, and they deliver results either on time or early. There are two important factors that influence the client's perception when rainmakers commit to perform. *First, rainmakers assume personal accountability for managing the initial engagements with new clients.* This allows them to mentor the engagement team personally, and it ensures quality control because it removes any uncertainties about what was committed—to whom and when.

Second, and perhaps more important, rainmakers are known for their ability to manage the expectations that their clients have about the results that will be delivered. Remember the phrase "Underpromise and overdeliver?" That phrase describes performance management quite well. A rainmaker's strategy is to be conservative when committing results to be delivered. Once a conservative expectation is set in a client's mind, it is easy to beat it. Most customer satisfaction problems we've seen arise because suppliers *overpromise and underdeliver.*

Rainmakers also break complex problems down into bite-sized pieces, so the scope of an initial engagement is more manageable than trying to solve the whole problem. Defining problems in small pieces also makes it easier for a client to do business with a verbal agreement. This is analogous to the way a contractor pours the foundation of a building first, thus making sure it is secure before building the other components of the structure that rest on top of it. (We'll explain more about that when we discuss why hitting singles instead of home runs is also a good idea.)

4. Conduct feedback meetings. Real estate selection boils down to location, location, location! Similarly, rainmaking boils down to communication, communication, communication! Quality is ensured when rainmakers keep their clients on the same page with them. They insist on holding team meetings to review progress as often as is practical, and they make sure that all parties who have an interest in the project attend. The client's sponsoring executive, the one who made the initial commitment, attends along with the rainmaker.

Rainmakers use the same facilitation skills in feedback meetings that they employ in interviews; in fact, all meetings are interviews to a rainmaker. They never stop digging for information, even when they are presenting results. The typical feedback meeting resembles the best brainstorming session you have ever attended. Rainmakers are very adept at introducing ideas through brainstorming, posing ideas as questions. (We'll cover more about this technique in Chapter 11.)

5. Uncover additional needs. A rainmaker's best-kept secret is to always be interest*ed*. This step in the Engagement Model is one of the many ways that this secret is put to practical use. Look carefully again at Figure 9.1. See how this step leads into additional engagements by considering what happened in steps 1 through 4? Let's review what has happened leading up to this point. First, the rainmaker helped a client identify a need by facilitating a *diagnosis of a problem;* next, client personnel participated in every aspect of *engagement creation;* results were then brainstormed during *feedback meetings;* finally, the team was positioned to decide how to broaden the solution by expanding the effort to other issues or areas. As with the construction contractor, the foundation of the building has been designed, and the team is ready to start working on the rest of the project.

A Rabbit in the Hat

A group of IBM people was describing to us the way a large consulting firm had seemingly taken over the information-processing strategy role in one of their large accounts. These folks had hardly noticed when a senior partner from the firm assembled a small team of the customer's staff members to brainstorm about information strategy. They soon became acutely aware that more and more of the customer's people were engaged in the strategy work. And they were shocked when the customer told them that all procurement decisions, including commitments reflected in the approved budget, would have to wait until the strategy work was completed. The IBM team said the customer was providing offices and conference room space for the consulting team, a perk that had never been offered to them. One of the IBM reps exclaimed, "A couple of consultants started this thing, but they've multiplied like rabbits! They're all over the place!"

Clients like the way rainmakers focus on their issues. One factor that allows consultants to multiply, while enhancing trust and respect, is the way their rainmakers break client issues into manageable pieces.

BASEBALL AND BIG SHIPS

The practice of breaking issues into pieces is analogous to baseball. Imagine that one of your sales reps uncovers a bid opportunity that has the potential for selling millions of dollars of your products and services. Many reps would call that kind of opportunity a *home run!* A deal like this is usually packaged very well by the customer, and most home runs are won or lost on such simple factors as pricing, financial terms, support, and delivery schedule. Traditional sales reps find lots of these deals because most large corporations and government agencies are very proactive about publishing their major procurements for the world to see.

Rainmakers walk away from home runs.

When presented with the opportunity to pursue a home run, an astute rainmaker will ask, "How does this customer know the project should cost $____ million? Who determined that figure?" Because the price and value have already been determined, the rainmaker would quickly discern that competition must be involved. Home runs are usually bidding situations in which all of the high profit margin work has already been done. Another rainmaker has likely facilitated the problem diagnosis in a home run and is helping the customer negotiate the best pricing and terms.

Staying with the baseball analogy, rainmakers prefer to hit *singles*. They like to put as many players on base (into the engagement) as possible. Practical experience has proven that customers never really know what will completely satisfy them at the beginning of a major undertaking. Think of the variables that can occur during a massive implementation project:

- Key people can be reassigned, or they may quit.
- Economic factors can affect any business decision. Large budget items are the first to fall under the axe in uncertain times.
- Products and technologies can become obsolete.
- Management can lose focus on a big project and forget why they started it in the first place.

A seasoned sales executive once told me how frustrated he had become because his salesforce was always trying to hit home runs, a practice that he said always put his forecast in jeopardy. He said that his folks always bet that a big ship would come in, and that few of them realized *big ships seldom come in.*

Engaging on a small part of a new project is like putting a man on first base. When the team uncovers additional needs, as shown in the Engagement Model, two men are on base. As the process keeps repeating itself, more runners get on base and score; it's better to hit a home run when the bases are full of runners. Waiting for the next home run is like waiting for the next big ship to come in. Singles keep the game moving constantly, and each new one with a client is often bigger than its predecessor. (Maybe baseball and shipping can be mixed after all!)

This singles' approach to business development has many advantages, the first being that it provides for risk sharing. Both rainmaker and client can easily commit to a small single for the initial engagement, often even doing so orally and thus providing an opportunity for a rainmaker to share the risk with the client. Remember that we spoke about *lose-win negotiations* when we discussed success factors? Rainmakers sometimes share risk by volunteering to waive their fees in the *diagnosis* stage. Sharing risk gets the ball rolling without incurring the complexities and legal headaches of negotiating win-win agreements.

Sharing risk this way is relatively easy to do because the financial impact is small, but savvy businesspeople, including rainmakers, wouldn't share the risk on a multi-million-dollar home run. Traditional sales organizations have a difficult time persuading their financial management officers to agree to share the risk on home runs. The bottom line is that client executives perceive that rainmakers routinely share risk whereas traditional suppliers don't. Executives like the feeling that their rainmaker's firm has "skin" in the game.

The second advantage inherent in hitting singles is that rainmakers have the option to disengage every time a piece of work is completed. They can stay for the next round or leave. Home runs entrap the suppliers contractually for the whole effort, even when they underestimate costs, manpower, or any other factors. Rainmakers get involved in big projects as they continue to uncover additional needs. When projects grow to a size that calls for a legal contract, rainmakers cover themselves with a process called "change control," whereby they advise a client at the beginning of the project that additional fees will be charged if the client changes any aspect of the project specifications at any time.

Clients don't object to this practice when they are informed about it in advance, and they like knowing they have the option to change something when it's appropriate.

The third and biggest advantage of singles is that they enhance mutual feelings of trust because multiple engagements give clients many fresh opportunities to watch the rainmakers with each new phase of a project. The clients get a chance to see the rainmakers performing over and over again. Credibility and trust are both enhanced when the Engagement Model has a chance to work.

TACTICS VERSUS STRATEGY

Let's run the Engagement Model the way a traditional sales organization would run it. The "Sales Engagement Process" in Figure 9.2 illustrates how different these two approaches as shown by the two models are. Notice that the sales process excludes diagnosing the client's problem, although sales calls and monologues have certainly occurred to arrive at this point. Lacking the step of diagnosis, the sales process begins with a bid response or proposal that probably calls for at least one sales presentation; and financial terms are also negotiated during this first phase. It's difficult to present any customized information if the customer's issue isn't clearly understood by the sales reps who will write the proposals.

Assuming the deal is sold, the next major event is to deliver the product to the customer, a step we call "installation." Most companies we've known bring the selling process to a close at this point, meaning that they exit here and consider the sales cycle complete. Many companies give recognition and bonuses to their people if they exit earlier than originally projected, and many customers are willing to pay a small premium for early delivery as well. On-time or early exits are believed to boost productivity.

Another popular traditional process that many companies employ after they exit an installation is a Customer Satisfaction Survey. These surveys are only useful when they are conducted after the salesforce has delivered or installed the product, because they ask customers, "How did we do?" Customers respond to the surveys by assigning numerical ratings to various aspects of the supplier's installation efforts, product quality, professional demeanor, and so on. Contrast this method of gath-

FIGURE 9.2 *The Sales Engagement Process*

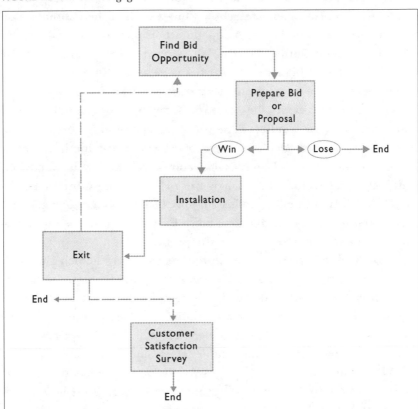

ering critical customer data to the way rainmakers do it in feedback meetings and by continuing to ask questions as they hit new singles.

We're not condemning these surveys. They provide much information that can be useful to various corporate functions. But we do question why so many companies rely on them as their primary postsale, customer contact vehicle. However you slice it, *rainmakers stick around whereas salespeople leave.*

You can receive perfect satisfaction scores on a survey without knowing the person who's rating you! I had experience with this during the years I spent as a vice president at Cisco Systems. A major portion of the executive bonus payment at Cisco depended on the company's ability to achieve high marks from customers on customer satisfaction targets that were set at the beginning of each fiscal year. A bonus was paid only if the targets were met or exceeded, and this bonus scheme kept every executive focused on customer satisfaction. One-twelfth of the customer base was surveyed monthly by an independent firm, and progress was reported frequently during the year. We were proud of the fact that our customers rated us higher each year than the year before.

A great deal of any customer's satisfaction was based on the quality of the technical support they received from our company. High-tech companies have long suffered the ire of their customers by providing inadequately staffed telephone support. (A client of mine in the early 1990s told me he thought Bill Gates's company's name was "Microsoft, Will You Please Hold!") To get away from that weakness, Internet commerce companies installed online support facilities so customers could dial in, report a problem, and get known fixes downloaded without having to speak to a representative on the phone.

Cisco's surveys revealed that customers who were helped electronically were much happier than customers who received their support from living, breathing representatives. If you combine this online support system with the rest of the online applications that drive an e-Commerce company's interaction with its customers, the rainmaker in me has to ask, "How can a relationship develop under these circumstances?"

Who would you guess responds to customer satisfaction surveys? CEOs? Presidents? Do any top-level managers or decision makers understand or take the time to answer the product and supplier-oriented questions that are asked in these surveys?

No! Companies delegate the responsibility for answering satisfaction surveys to the employees who install, maintain, and use the inquisitive vendor's support. An online technical support process produces tremendous gains in productivity as well as great customer satisfaction survey results, but do the companies that are dependent on these systems understand that they may be sacrificing opportunities to create trusted relationships? It doesn't appear that way. Customer satisfaction surveys simply cannot replace face-to-face feedback from executives, nor can they replace the level of dialogue made possible by the Pyramid.

Our customer satisfaction survey discussion is not intended as pure criticism. Rather, we include it as a cautionary speed bump for readers who want to develop rainmaker attributes. Internet and e-commerce solutions often dehumanize business relationships. We want to *re*humanize them.

ASSIGNMENT

Here's an assignment for those of you willing to step up and try a little rainmaking. Think about it: Rainmakers are curious people by nature. That's one reason why they prefer to ask questions. Rainmakers will be interested in you if they're given the opportunity to meet you. It should be easy to find out who the senior-level rainmaker is that mentors your customer's teams.

Have one of your most senior executives call that rainmaker to ask for an appointment to discuss ways that your two firms can work together. You may find that a customer team is in need of some expertise that one of your employees possesses, and that may spell out an opportunity for you to get involved with problem diagnosis on the team. That's the way collaborative opportunities present themselves, and companies like yours can uncover them easily if you try.

SUMMARY

The Engagement Model illustrates how rainmakers create and build relationships by delivering solid results to their clients. The cycle begins with a diagnosis of a client's problem that is led by a credible rainmaker, and trust develops as additional engagements are created. There is no end game, no exit point in the cycle. Every step in the process is driven by the rainmaker's interpersonal skills and ability to facilitate effective teamwork with a client's personnel.

Though your company is probably not ready to adopt this entire model yet, you can start its implementation by helping a handful of selected customers diagnose some of the issues that will drive their product decisions. Try giving them a checkup.

10

QUESTIONS

We appreciate people more for the questions they ask us than for the information they present!

Do you know how to ask good questions? Of course you do! You do it all the time with friends, relatives, children, your spouse, significant other, business partners, and other people who occupy a special place in your life. You are comfortable with those people because they don't intimidate you, and you don't feel as though you have to perform for them. You are interested in them. Feelings of mutual trust probably come naturally with these people.

Here's a different spin on the same question. Do you ask your customers good questions, the kinds of questions that enable the same feelings of mutual trust that you feel with friends? Rainmakers learn to ask good questions to get the wheels spinning in their interviews. Our task at this point is to define *good* as it relates to the topic of questions. At the conclusion of this chapter, you'll appreciate the way rainmakers distinguish themselves from salespeople and build trust by virtue of the questions they ask.

THE WRONG QUESTIONS

Our discussion and beliefs about what constitutes "good questions" is offered in the context of rainmaker behavior. The goal of questioning, in this context, is to open a dialogue from which a trusted relationship can evolve. Let's look first at the types of questions that would *not* work in an initial interview. Rainmakers avoid asking the following types of questions:

Rhetorical questions. These are questions that *The American Heritage Dictionary* (New College ed.) defines as those "to which no answer is expected, or to which only one answer may be made." Many of the techniques taught in sales training methods are based on these questions. Most of us are offended when asked an obvious question that needs no answer, yet salespeople are trained to do that. The theory is that asking any question will cause reps to appear interested in their customers. Rhetorical questions are comfortable to ask because any response to them will not be controversial. Still, customers feel manipulated by them.

Trick questions. Years ago, many high-tech companies taught sales reps to probe for the answers to big questions by asking lots of little ones. For example, if a rep was unsure if a customer planned to order a computer system, the rep was taught to ask, "Are you going to order your system in blue or red?" Another favorite approach was to ask questions about the facilities, such as, "Will your current computer room handle the additional electrical and air-conditioning loads?" Another approach: "How soon will you be needing the equipment?" All of these questions were meant to entrap the customer into revealing whether a purchase was going to be made. Would customers prefer to be asked a direct question, such as, "Are you going to order our system?" You decide!

Other trick question techniques teach reps how to imply the answers they are seeking within the questions they ask. For example, if you have authored an online financial accounting system and are involved in a sales call on a manager whose company has suffered from poor financial data, you could ask, "What kinds of investments in Internet-based software solutions do you think you could make today that would prevent financial reporting errors next year?" The answer is obvious— "Internet-based software solutions"—and almost rhetorical.

Shopworn questions. Sales reps from every industry have been taught to ask the following three questions: (1) How is your business doing this year? (2) Can you tell me your top three critical success factors? (3) Will you please tell me the top two or three things that keep you awake at night?

Our experience tells us that these three questions or similar ones are easily brushed aside, because customers are either amused or offended by them. Regardless of which question is asked, the person asking hasn't earned the right to ask it.

In the Wheel of Fortune in Chapter 6, we disclosed how rainmakers invest their personal time researching clients before conducting the first interview. They find that the quality of their interviews depends on the quality of the questions they ask, and the quality of the questions depends on the quantity and quality of data they can obtain about the clients in their research.

Remember this: Good research leads to good questions; zero research leads to rhetorical, trick, or shopworn questions, or to no questions at all.

CLOSED QUESTIONS AND A QUID PRO QUO

Unless you've lived in a cave for the past 50 years, you know the difference between open and closed questions. Closed questions evoke a monosyllabic response such as yes, no, 12, 40 percent, and the like. These questions have a proper place in a dialogue, but that place is not at the beginning of a conversation. Unfortunately, some salespeople learn to use closed questions to manipulate their victims into giving predictable responses. An example would be the questions we have learned to anticipate, with a lot of trepidation, from the automobile salesman we mentioned earlier. Let's listen again to a pure salesman at work:

If I can get the boss to sell you this car at our cost, will you buy it from me today?

One can barely grunt an answer to this type of question because the only responses possible are *yes, no, maybe, or no response at all.* This technique is also known as quid pro quo, which means "something for something." It asks the buyer to take action if the condition of selling the car at cost is met. The question really asks, "If I do *this,* will you do *that* in return?" Many of us learned with the purchase of our first car that accepting the quid pro quo results in the car agency's manager saying *no* to the deal. Undaunted by their manager's refusal, auto sales reps keep the signed contracts on the table, using them to begin the real negotiation for what is the achievable price. When you're in the middle of a situation like this, it's hard to remember that it all started with a simple closed question, the mainstay of classical sales behavior because it allows the person asking the question to keep control of the conversation.

If you have a specific agenda and are hell-bent on following it, opening a dialogue that you don't control is probably not a comfortable prospect. Can you imagine an auto salesman approaching you to ask, "What are the factors that influence your selection when you decide to buy an automobile?" That kind of question could lead just about anywhere, and few auto sales reps have the confidence or patience to allow that to happen. Remember, they operate on the theory that they have only one chance to close a deal with you, and that chance occurs within the first 30 minutes. If you leave the showroom without making a purchase, you'll most likely never return, at least to that showroom.

The most common quid pro quo questioning technique employed by sales reps from typical commercial businesses sounds like this:

> *If I can show you a way to_____, will you_____?*
> If I can *show you a way to collect your accounts receivable 20 days faster than you are collecting them today,* will you *purchase my solution?*
> If I can *prove to you that our device reduces emissions by 50 percent,* will you *buy it?*
> If I can *show you a way to cure cancer and solve world hunger,* will you *participate?*

When was the last time you were on the receiving end of questions like these? Did you feel a hidden trap was awaiting you if you took the bait and answered?

The inherent problem buried within these questions is that they are argumentative. They set up a win-lose scenario, because the salesperson is really asking, "If I can prove my point, will you drop yours?"

Another problem with asking *"If I can,"* is that it turns the spotlight on the person asking the question. It creates within the customer the expectation of a performance, because once approval to show him or her something is granted, the salesperson had better show it. Asking "If I can show you a way" is like saying "Watch me do this" or "Catch this performance."

OPEN QUESTIONS AND DIALOGUE CREATION

The word *dialogue* comes from two Greek roots, *dia*—meaning "through" or "with each other"—and *logos*—meaning "the word." Dialogue then is "meaning flowing through words." Its goal is to open new ground by establishing a field for inquiry in which people can become more aware of the context around their experience and the thought and feeling that created the experience. As we practice dialogue, we pay attention to the spaces between the words, the timing of the words, and the timbre and tone of voice, and we listen for the meaning.

GOOD QUESTIONS

Keep the preceding thoughts about dialogues in mind as we look at the kinds of questions that are considered "good" by rainmakers. It should come as no surprise that rainmakers prefer *open questions* when they want to start a dialogue. As mentioned in the context of television interviewers, rainmakers succeed by adhering to the following rule: *The best questions are those that prompt the other person to talk.*

What's Love Got to Do with It?

The ideas we're about to introduce are everywhere it seems. Author Dr. James Dobson flirts with rainmaking when he defines *love* as "giving somebody your undivided attention." In his recent book titled *Raising Boys*, Dobson stresses the significance of what he calls "the first five minutes" in a dialogue with someone important. Speaking almost like a rainmaker, Dobson asserts, "Fortunately, whenever we begin a new interaction, we have a chance to reset the mood."

If you are an aspiring rainmaker who approaches a customer executive these days, you will most certainly have some mood resetting to do to start a meaningful dialogue. Both you and the customer executive come to the table with baggage. The customer is expecting a performance, and you are incredibly anxious about your ability to please the customer, who is expecting you to perform.

TWO TYPES OF OPEN QUESTIONS

The best way to reset a mood and eliminate baggage carried by you and a customer is to show your sincere interest in your customer from the first moment of the conversation by asking an open question that proves you are there to listen and learn, not to manipulate, trick, or perform. The two types of open questions on which rainmakers focus—*content* and *process*—prompt two very different kinds of responses.

Content Questions

These are questions that ask about the ingredients or the contents of something and go something like this:

> *We are aware that you have implemented a new Internet-based supply chain management system. What information are you currently managing with that system?*

This *content question* passes the test for being open because it elicits a detailed, perhaps even lengthy, response about the contents of the new system. It definitely has the potential to prompt the other person to talk, and it's a better choice than a closed question that may ask, "How many departments are using the new system?" This closed question would prompt an answer like "Four."

Here's another example of a content question:

> *What are the names of all of the agencies that are supported by my contribution to this charity? If you don't know all of them, will you please tell me who the top five or six are?*

Another business example would be:

Will you please run through the main reasons for your decision?

Content questions, like closed questions, are effective and necessary ingredients in a dialogue, but neither represents the best way to start one, because the answers to content questions tend to be *quantitative.* They don't allow *qualitative* information, feelings, or facts to be shared unless the respondent takes the initiative to force qualitative responses. Sergeant Joe Friday on the long-running television series *Dragnet* was famous for asking content questions, exhorting his suspects to give him "the facts. Just give me the facts."

One reason rainmakers are so cautious about the questions they ask is that their goal is to always convey respect for the people they interview. Respect is obviously a main ingredient in developing trust with another person, and the questions we ask—and the way we ask them—can backfire if we're not sincerely interest*ed* in the answers we get back.

People are basically respectful of others. They will answer your questions,
so you may as well ask questions that will start the dialogue you are
seeking.

Discussion about respect leads to another reason why you should *not* open an interview with a *content question.* When they come out of the blue, these questions may appear to be a test or pop quiz that requires the other person to recite chapter and verse about a topic. Content questions can backfire on the interviewer if the other person doesn't know all the facts. Remember, a primary goal in any interview is to establish mutual feelings of comfort that can lead to trust. Putting people on the spot by asking them to perform is not comfortable, especially if they don't know the facts you're seeking.

Executives are usually generalists and prefer to deal with qualitative information. They slurp the sauce and enjoy it without wanting to get into the details of the recipe. Executives don't like to be criticized for the way they do their homework if they get an A in the course! Whatever their individual makeup or time constraints, executives don't have the time or inclination to work with many details. That's one reason they will often accept help with the business issues that trouble them.

One way to make another person feel at ease is to ask a question about a topic that you know falls within his or her area of interest or expertise. Knowing enough to ask such an appropriate question in this context leads back to our Wheel of Fortune discussion about research. This next type of question has proven to be the most effective option for opening an interview.

Process Questions

Rather than probing for ingredients, *process questions* ask about the actions invoked or the steps taken when addressing a situation. These kinds of questions enable respondents to explain what they do when they are successful or what they do when solving issues and problems. Process questions also allow people to demonstrate their knowledge about something they know well. The basic question being asked is: "What do you do when you do that?"

Start with context. A good process question starts with what we call a "context statement." This is the question's introduction, and it reveals just a little bit about the rainmaker's experience, capabilities, and the time the rainmaker invested in research prior to the visit. It is short, sweet, and to the point. Here's an example of a context statement:

> *We have been helping our clients in the manufacturing industry create supply chain processes and systems for the past decade. The research we have done on your company suggests that you are grappling with many of the same issues our other clients have faced. Specifically, we read that some of your suppliers have not followed guidelines for your processes and systems, resulting in some critical inventory shortages.*

Note that the interviewer has used real data about this customer and has also shown some degree of industry knowledge without focusing too long on himself. The following process question flows very easily from that preamble:

> *As the CEO of this company, what are the steps you are taking to address this issue?*

That's it! That's a process question! Does it seem too easy? Do you want to make it more complex than it is? Assuming that the research is accurate, any rainmaker will hit the bull's-eye with this kind of question. Most executives would answer it. Wouldn't you?

Most sales executives and sales reps that we've coached over the years have been uncomfortable with this entire concept at first. We figured out long ago that their concern is twofold. First, the question doesn't direct the customer to answer in any specific way. Second, time may be wasted if the customer's answer doesn't conform to the rep's agenda, namely, the product that has been predestined as the solution. Yes, this question is 180 degrees away from a sales process question.

T h e   H e a l t h   C a r e   I n t e r v i e w

The following true story relates an interview I conducted a few years ago when I was VP of Marketing for a videoconferencing company in Austin, Texas. Our sales team invited me to attend a presentation they were scheduled to make to the CEO of one of the largest U.S. health care companies. My rainmaker's antenna rose when I heard the word presen- tation, *because I knew that no one from our company had ever met the CEO. Our team was anxious to prove that videoconferencing could help this customer save effort and money when acquiring hospitals. We wanted to show how airplane tickets and phone calls could be replaced by face-to-face meetings using teleconferencing.*

I conducted a review with the team prior to making the trip. They had done a pretty good job of researching facts about the customer, and the one fact that stood out above all the rest had to do with an issue the customer had with the hospitals they acquired. In a nutshell, we discovered that physicians didn't like the idea of becoming remote locations in a big chain, preferring to work under local control, where they could have a strong influence on policies. We were also aware that this company used one of our competitor's videoconferencing products, primarily for training classes.

Armed with this information, I cut the number of our participants for this meeting from seven or eight down to two of us and then prepared a process question that went something like this:

Mr. _____, we are amazed at the way you have been able to turn this company into the largest of its kind in the USA. We

*are curious about one thing. Our research, which included inter-
views with several of your managers, pointed to the difficulties
you are experiencing with retaining key physicians in the hospitals you are acquiring (Context).*

How do you deal with that issue as CEO? (Process question)

It was obvious that the CEO wasn't expecting that kind of question
right out of the gate. He thought for a moment and then asked why we
wanted to know that. Leaning back on my rainmaker experience, I told
him we were interested in the success he had demonstrated and would like
to know a little more about it. In James Dobson's words, we had to "reset
the mood."

The CEO answered the question. He took us through the things he
personally did on announcing an acquisition. The steps included traveling to the remote area, meeting with the key physicians, assuring them of
his personal interest in their happiness, and then keeping in touch with
them on a frequent basis after the initial meeting.

He paused after several minutes and asked if we'd heard enough.
He was clearly enjoying the opportunity to talk about himself. That's a
natural reaction because he was the only person on the planet that could
answer our question. He had given us a fairly detailed accounting of the
steps he took throughout his involvement with acquisitions, and he
seemed impressed that we were tuned in to his issue with physicians. Had
we been consultants, we would have created the perfect opportunity to pursue possible ways we could help reengineer his process. But we weren't consultants! We were traditional sales and marketing folks who now had an
opportunity to try to bring videoconferencing into the CEO's world. This
is one of many personal experiences that convince me business executives
can become rainmakers.

We began asking more focused, specific questions regarding the CEO's
process. We asked how much time was involved in traveling to remote
locations, and he replied, "Too much!" We asked him if he dared delegate
the matter to his staff members, and he said that was out of the question.
We finally got around to asking what kind of help he needed, and he
was open to suggestions. Our suggestion was videoconferencing, and the
discussion went on from there. The situation ultimately resulted in an
order.

Go back and reread our process question carefully—then read it a second time. Now, be just as attentive as you read the following statement. I want you to look carefully at the way a traditional salesperson would have started this same interaction with the CEO:

Mr. _____, we want to thank you for taking time out of your busy schedule to see us this morning. We know your time is valuable, so we'll be brief. We represent an Austin, Texas, company engaged in marketing videoconferencing systems. Our systems are well known in your industry because they are built on a standard PC platform that allows them to be easily integrated into the fabric of your information-processing strategy.

You are currently using one of our competitor's products in your training department, but your information-processing managers tell us that you can't integrate your current video products into the rest of your systems, and thus your investment in videoconferencing is not protected.

We would like to show you why most of your competitors have switched to our products. But first, would you share with us your CEO perspective on the top priorities that you are addressing this year?

There could be as many variations on this opening monologue as there are sales reps to deliver it. But I think this is a pretty close generalization of what a typical sales rep would have said to open that meeting.

Can you see the difference? More important, can you see how the sales rep's method takes the CEO out of his comfort zone immediately? (We never met a top-level executive who knew or cared what a PC platform was!) We got the CEO engaged in an application discussion that found its way into many discussions in his Information Processing Department, and those discussions clearly had his sponsorship.

Where would the sales approach have landed? Would this technique have uncovered the physician retention issue? At what point in the sales monologue do you think the CEO would have thought to himself, "Hmm, this is a sales call about videoconferencing. How did these guys slip past my managers down there? They don't seem impressed with our current systems that represent a bunch of money. Are they disparaging our current vendor? Did we do a poor job in our evaluation?"

Let me qualify our example with a couple of thoughts. Being a rainmaker worked because, as leader of the effort, I was a vice president of our company. A stronger relationship would have probably developed if our CEO, or perhaps one of our board members, made the initial approach. We still executed the meeting with an executive matchup. I doubt that our sales reps could have pulled it off even if they understood how to execute the right skills. The packaging of the right interpersonal skills along with a Pyramid coverage plan works for businesses that are willing to change their approach and act more like rainmakers.

Don't Ask If You Don't Care

If you are going to ask good questions, you have to be prepared to listen, really listen, to the answers that come back to you. Asking process questions like a rainmaker signals that you are sincerely interested in the answer and in the person giving it. I know you have encountered someone who has asked you a question only to forget to pay close attention to your answer because she was formulating the next question to ask you. Isn't it frustrating to give a sincere answer to what you believed to be a sincere question, only to have the other person ignore your response and ask you something else? You can tell when others are formulating instead of listening by watching their eyes and body language after they have asked a question. Some sales reps have been taught that asking questions, any question, is enough to satisfy a step in their process. People feel manipulated when confronted with this behavior.

Why Ask at All?

I attended the annual shareholders' meeting for a large retail conglomerate in the Midwest. The company had reported a bad year; its market share was dwindling and its financials stunk. After the chairman of the company had given an overview, he announced that the company would entertain questions from the audience. This was a first for this company, and the chairman said they really wanted to hear from their shareholders at the meeting, many of whom were long-standing and loyal franchisees.

A remote microphone was passed to a gentleman in the middle of the crowd. After announcing he was a loyal franchisee, he asked, "If things are going as well as you say, why isn't the company making any money?" Heads turned toward the man amid a general chorus of "Um-hums." It seemed as though many others had come to the meeting with the same concern in mind

The chairman looked right at the guy, smiled, and said, "That was an excellent question!" Then he immediately looked out at the audience and said, "That's a great question! Who has another one?" The next person to speak asked the same question with a slightly different spin, and he also received kudos from the chairman for asking an excellent question. The chairman wrapped up that segment of the program by thanking the two gentlemen for their questions and then told the corporate secretary to be sure to include questions in all future meetings! He never responded to the questions!

This story is both preposterous and true. It is unfortunate that this kind of rude behavior happens every day in business settings where people don't listen to the responses others offer to their questions. The right reason to ask is to obtain an answer. Any other reason is transparent to the person being asked.

ALIGNMENT

Asking good questions and then listening to the answers puts both rainmaker and customer on the same page—it aligns them—in a dialogue. Try to remember your first dialogue with your spouse, significant other, a new friend, or perhaps a new employer. Chances are those dialogues were not superficial. Most of us ask very good questions when we are trying to get to know someone. It works the same way in business for rainmakers, and it can work that way for you.

Dialogues become productive when both parties feel aligned with each other in the conversation. *Alignment* allows emotions and actions to be synced with the words that are exchanged when a question-and-answer dialogue occurs. The PAR Group does a terrific job of explaining alignment in their leadership and teamwork materials. PAR represents emotions and actions as ten rungs on a ladder, each rung linking an emotional feeling to a physical response as the ladder ascends from negative at the bottom to neutral and finally to positive.

Time doesn't allow a detailed discussion of all ten rungs here, so we'll just consider the negative, neutral, and positive zones for now. At the lowest level (negative), a person will be indifferent to you and the questions you are asking and may appear troubled or fearful at this stage or even hostile. Hostility shows a level of engagement and can be dealt with more easily than indifference.

When in neutral mode, a person may challenge you a little bit but will appear open to listening to what you have to ask or say. People at neutral may appear reserved, but they are usually open to pursuing a dialogue that is offered to them.

People in the positive zone make it obvious they are wholeheartedly engaged with your topic and answer your questions willingly. Our health care CEO engaged immediately around our questioning about physician retention. We can't emphasize enough the degree to which good research makes possible questions that prompt positive emotional responses. You'll know when people are in a positive zone with you because they will appear enthusiastic and confident, and will seem willing to commit themselves to a constructive dialogue with you. The PAR Group makes the point that confident commitment is the emotional action that any conversationalist should seek in a dialogue. We believe this signals the beginning stage of trust.

According to PAR, alignment is achieved only if questions are asked at the level appropriate to where the customer is on the ladder. Asking CEOs specific questions about information-processing plans or systems may cause them to slide downward on the ladder into negative territory, because they may be fearful of displaying ignorance. If research reveals that a company is in the midst of a financial crisis, it's probably best to ask a CEO or CFO about something else to prevent driving them down the ladder. The financial issues will surface under their own power once the relationship is established.

The key to creating alignment is to listen carefully to an answer and then respond by acknowledging, through your own emotions, words, and actions, that you understand the other person's point of view.

HOMEWORK: A PERSONAL EXPERIENCE WITH NONALIGNMENT

My son recently received a grade of 89 in math for one marking period, one point below the 90 required for an A. All of his other grades were above 90, so the 89 resulted in his missing the straight A honor roll. My boy was definitely below neutral regarding what he perceived to be a tragedy. I consider myself a practitioner of alignment, but in this case I blew it! The first thing I did was say, "Hey, 89 is a pretty good score," thereby invalidating his feelings. If I should have learned just one lesson in life by now, it would be:

Don't try to lighten another man's load by being a cheerleader when he's down!

My son fumed even more at my response and I could see him sliding down the ladder. I tried to recover by asking him this process question: "What do you think you could have done differently that would have resulted in a 90?" He told me that he had blown one lousy homework assignment. I followed this revelation by asking him, "Would you believe that being the best of the best means that you can never let down, and that'll be the case in your whole life as well?" At that point I was toast!

I can see, in retrospect, how I went from being a positive cheerleader to a neutral inquisitor and finally to a negative anchor around his neck in three easy steps! None of my actions were appropriate, and we were never aligned in our brief conversation. What my son needed was empathy from me. He needed to know that I had been there and done that as well. He needed a hug.

Hitting a troubled or fearful person with supreme confidence is like kicking them when they are down.

My interpersonal train wreck can be directly correlated with some of the business situations we have seen where two people try to converse about something when they are not properly aligned. The best examples of this kind of poor alignment occur when salespeople try to present their solutions to businesspeople who haven't yet acknowledged that they have a problem.

We've seen many worst-case scenarios where customer meetings have blown up because the parties were not aligned. This often happens for two main reasons:

1. A sales rep discovers a major problem that a customer is experiencing and reports the problem to the customer in a packaged presentation that includes a solution. Earlier we had cautioned against trying to define someone else's problems in a vacuum without facilitating the problem owner's participation in the process. Omitting the problem owner's participation bombs, because the presenters usually haven't earned the right to hold an opinion, and their opinions are seldom taken seriously. Sometimes it doesn't pay to be right even when you are right!

2. The person making an approach cannot conduct the conversation with true empathy because he or she has never walked in the same shoes, has never held the same position, and has never had to wrestle with the same issues. Yet this person will plow into an empathetic-sounding monologue for want of anything else to say. Rainmakers mitigate this situation because they have either faced the same issues in their role as business owner or they have seen the issues through the eyes of other client executives. We've said many times, perhaps ad nauseam, that *executives prefer to talk to executives.*

SUMMARY

Rainmakers exhibit sincere interest in their clients by thoughtfully preparing and asking questions. Emphasis should be placed on "thoughtful preparation," which requires investing time performing research on a client. Time taken in preparation provides an opportunity to learn about the client, and rainmakers, like all of us, can only prepare good process questions when armed with research information. Once prepared, rainmakers use their interrogative skills to open a dialogue based on issues that surfaced during the research. Content questions and closed questions are used to keep dialogue flowing but don't work for starting a dialogue.

Rainmakers avoid the trivial questioning techniques often employed in traditional sales training courses. Rather than using questions in a manipulative way, they seek answers that will ultimately help them decide if they are willing and able to help the other person. They don't try to impress clients by the sheer number of questions they ask, and they listen carefully to the answers to their questions. These actions align with the client and the client's issue.

We believe that you set your company up for failure if you read this book and then assume that your sales department can execute process questions appropriately with your customers' executives. Yes, anyone at any level can ask process questions, which can help sales reps and other employees hold their own in executive meetings. But sales reps should utilize these ideas where they can be effective. Sadly, millions of executives and managers have "drunk the Kool-Aid" that's offered by sales trainers and CRM technology providers, so they are accustomed to delegating every new idea about customer relationships to their salesforces. If you are an executive, please consider the benefits that will accrue to your company, as well as to you personally, if you'll become a mentor of these ideas instead of delegating them.

Many executives have actually thanked us when we finished interviewing them. One top executive told us, "Thanks for coming in here today. Seems like everybody that comes through my door wants to tell me what I should do or how they can do it for me. You're the first guys who have asked me what I think needs to be done, and I appreciate that." You will find yourself getting these kinds of kudos too.

11

GO EAST!

It's time to organize the previous chapters into actionable steps for those of you who want to develop your ability and the ability of your organization to create trusted relationships with customers. The metaphor we are about to introduce should tie up the loose ends we've created, giving you a practical means by which to plan for and execute your first executive interview. Traditional business leaders who master this process may experience some fundamental changes in the way they ultimately lead their organization into deeper customer relationships. Believe us! Your first successful interview will change forever the way you approach your customers.

A friend who works for one of the largest and most successful consulting companies specializing in CRM (customer relationship management) and other Internet-based systems' implementations heard about our effort to write this book. He asked me about the theme and contents one day at the golf course, so I gave him a brief overview. He chuckled and said, "Good luck! All you're trying to do is change 100 years of business behavior!" Turning serious for a moment, he followed with, "The corporate clients I have worked with need to hear that message, but only a small percentage of them would actually implement it. You are suggesting monumental change."

We beg to differ with my friend because we've seen executives and managers successfully make the journey. This discussion always brings us back to the subject of cultural change. Many of our beliefs and habits are so ingrained that we are scarcely aware of them. Below is a humorous personal example about the difficulties involved in conducting a major change.

Consulting partnerships, working through their rainmakers, pursue trusted relationships easily because their cultures encourage—no, demand—it. We hope that you are getting an appreciation for your own potential to make changes in the way you approach and think about your customers. We remind you that our goal is to give you enough information to help you and other members of your organization imitate and implement many of a rainmaker's characteristics.

You can increase your focus on building interpersonal skills; on developing a pyramid coverage plan for your accounts; and on developing deeper customer relationships where you have a reasonable shot at being trusted advisors. Let's turn now to the centerpiece of our work: the Diagnostic Compass.

C a t s   a n d   P a r a d i g m s

I have always disliked cats and have often joked about these little feline creatures. But I never realized the extent to which I'd made my dislike obvious until my three-year-old son asked my wife, "Mommy, when Daddy dies, can we get a cat?" We laughed, but I also filed the incident away in my memory, because it was a perfect example of how tightly we often hold on to opinions, biases, and old habits.

We assume that many of your corporate behaviors are just as ingrained as my dislike for cats, which is why companies continue to change sales training methods programs every year or two. Changing methodologies only deals with the symptoms and provides no real cure for the problems. The most generalized of these corporate "habits" is teaching sales reps to be effective at calling on executives.

THE DIAGNOSTIC COMPASS

Rainmakers have cornered the market on client-focused interpersonal attributes because business leaders have allowed it to happen. Businesses have been presenting at the same time rainmakers have been asking! Let's look at a fresh approach that can get you started on the road to change in your next meeting with a peer-level customer executive. A simple compass serves as a great metaphor to describe the interaction that occurs in a rainmaker's executive meeting. This is the way we would encourage you to behave when you schedule your first executive interview.

A compass always points north regardless of how you hold it. You will notice that north on our compass in Figure 11.1 represents the customer's issue. A good interviewer will be relentless in pursuing this issue during any conversation, and that's especially important in the first encounter. Remember that as a new rainmaker, you have to reset the mood that precedes you in most, if not all, of your current customer relationships, because you will be expected to come in and talk about yourself and your agenda.

FIGURE 11.1 *The Diagnostic Compass*

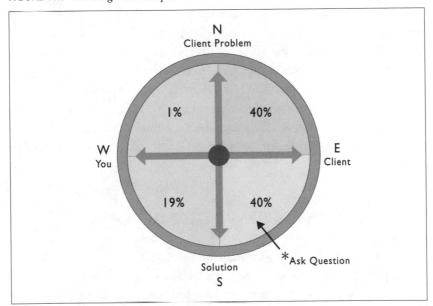

How do you begin your meeting in a way that signals to the customer executive that you are a different type of person than he was expecting? You start by asking a well-researched process question, wait for the answer, and then respond.

Bingo! You start the conversation with an irrepressible focus on the other person. Believe us when we tell you that centuries of human nature development are on your side. Your interviewee will be more comfortable when you ask about a topic he or she understands than if you talk about something *you* know.

Here are a couple of practical suggestions to keep in mind as you begin this fantastic interpersonal odyssey.

The executive may not answer your question directly but may ask why you are asking about your chosen subject. Respond confidently in a way that shows you are asking your question because you are interested in the answer. It's OK to simply say, "Because I'm interested in how you do that." Remember what we said about trying to fake interest? If you are not truly interested in getting an answer to your question, abort the meeting and send in another of your executives who *is* interested! If you are the VP of manufacturing, meet with someone from manufacturing, logistics, or distribution. Let your CFO meet with the financial executives, for example, and so on.

Some people need a few seconds to read the situation when the mood is being reset. They may offer no answer or no reaction at first. Silence is golden in these cases. Many aspiring rainmakers fail during this initial silence and feel they have to fill up the dead space with conversation. Remember this: You have to give the other person a chance to reset with you. If the other person has been anticipating a presentation or pitch, he'll be caught off balance by your interest. Time can be your ally in these cases if you can discipline yourself to *shut up and wait for the answer!*

HOW AND WHY TO GO EAST

Once you have asked your question(s) and the executive has begun to respond, keep your eyes, ears, and body language focused and involved with what you are hearing. East on our compass represents the *client*, the person you are interviewing. Once you have started your dialogue, you can go only east or west. We hope you'll see the wisdom in going east as this explanation unfolds.

East is where your relationship focus will connect with the customer or you'll stumble, because this is when you'll either establish a personal connection with the person (the other human being) seated before you or you'll blow it. The degree to which you connect will be obvious very quickly in the conversation. Your ability to connect will depend on the appropriateness of your questions and on the degree to which the customer believes that you are truly interest*ed* in the ways this issue impacts the customer personally. The first positive step toward alignment is connecting with one of the customer's top issues.

Think about recent conversations you've had with friends or loved ones. We're willing to bet that both you and the person you were talking to went east seamlessly with no bumps in the road. This phenomenon happens so naturally with people we're comfortable with that we often take it for granted. We ask process questions in these dialogues with friends, often beginning with such phrases as, "How did you fall into this mess? How have you been dealing with it? Take me through it again, step by step." Sound familiar? Those process questions seek the steps that have occurred. Why we've been coached throughout our business training that this kind of dialogue doesn't belong in business remains one of life's great mysteries.

Think about some of the phrases that you've heard ad infinitum: "Don't take things so personally." "Leave personalities out of it." "If you don't focus on your agenda, the customer certainly won't." "This is not a social club." Our favorite: "Keep your friendships out of business!" Yes, we've been coached to focus on our agenda, keep the ball in play, not allow ourselves to be distracted by personal stuff, and a host of other clichés. I once worked for an executive at Data General who liked to tell me, "We've got to make quota, and we don't have time to make friends out there!"

Going east means connecting with the other person, treating him or her as a *person*. You truly go east when you develop as much interest in the other person as you develop in the person's issue. Rainmaking requires knowing both the issue and the person who has it; we're not suggesting you invite a customer to your next birthday party, but you *can* connect personally with a customer in a manner that's appropriate in business.

Rainmakers learned long ago that those of us in traditional businesses happily leave all the "personal stuff" to them. They go to the bank knowing that we've got to meet our productivity targets. Taking time for the "mushy stuff" takes too long and doesn't translate into orders. We can't begin to count the number of sales executives who have passed on the opportunity to become rainmakers because they said they perceived getting involved with customers on a personal basis would lengthen their sales cycles. CRM systems encourage sales professionals to shorten, rather than lengthen, sales cycles. These same sales executives are always surprised to learn that focusing on the "mushy stuff" enables rainmakers to operate with extremely short cycles when they are working with new prospects. Yes, people will do bigger and better business deals with you when they trust you, and that kind of business sticks on the books longer.

The reason your personal conversations with friends proceed so easily in this easterly direction is that you leave your own agenda at the door when you talk to each other. Rainmakers do the same thing with clients, albeit they are always seeking to develop new business. Rainmakers know that their goal in every conversation with any client is to start a new relationship or to further develop an existing one. Here are two tips that may help you focus correctly as you lead your interview dialogue to the east:

1. *Leave your agenda at the door.* That includes leaving promotional materials, product descriptions, and company information in your briefcase in your car.
2. *Don't take notes.* Many sales reps have been trained to take notes, and some have even been coached to ask permission to do this. Taking notes when you are expressing sincere interest in another person is distracting. Your goal is to find out whether you and your customer can establish some common ground for further action. You can write all the notes to yourself that are necessary after the interview, perhaps in the parking lot if you have doubts about your ability to remember what people say in an important conversation.

Taking notes makes people feel they're participating in a survey. I remember sitting through a sales call in my office at Cisco with a sales rep from a PR firm. Every time I said something she would pause, look down, and write something. It was so distracting that I finally asked her what she was writing, and she replied, "Nothing really!" My secretary came in several times to interrupt our meeting and had a good vantage point to look over the rep's shoulder. After the meeting I asked what she had observed on the rep's writing pad, and she replied, "Doodling!"

I believe that sales reps take notes as a cover for brief time-outs when they formulate more thoughts and questions. I sometimes wonder if these people took a notepad to the candlelit dinner table when they shared a first romantic moment with their spouse or significant other. The dialogue probably went something like this:

> *"What do you do in your spare time?"*
> *"Well, I like to travel and I also like to cook."*
> *"Wow! Do you mind if I write that down in my notes?"*

Go back to the interview described earlier with the health care company's CEO. How did that situation differ from a romantic candle-lit dinner? A rainmaker would say there's no difference in behavior as long as the proper respect is shown the CEO. Giving executives the bum's rush (violating their personal space too quickly before you've earned the right to get close to them) can get you thrown out just as quickly as a candle-lit dinner can be interrupted when the object of your affection feels you are moving too quickly. There's a line there that you have to sense and feel as you proceed with your interviewing. That shouldn't present any problems if you are sincerely watching, focusing, and listening to what's being offered.

EAST LEADS TO SOUTH

When people become comfortable with you, they invite you in to stay a while—in rainmaking and in life. An executive who's willing to go east with you will usually warm to the flow of conversation and want to contribute. In the great majority of interviews, you needn't worry how to get executives to talk. Rather, you may need to worry about how to stop them once they get into a groove! It's no wonder. People like to talk about themselves, and executives are people. You, the rainmaker, are merely enabling them to speak.

At some point you do have to do some of the talking, but that necessitates changing the flow of the conversation. The flow in an interview changes naturally when the interviewee eventually gets tired of doing all of the talking. People who have done a lot of talking eventually come to a pause, look you in the eye, and ask what you think. Or they may ask you if you have experience that can add value to solving their issue. At this point the flow has changed. But be careful here! We'll show you why.

This change in conversational flow is a critical point in an interview. Because south on the compass is titled "Solution," many new rainmakers blow it here because they think this is the time when they should show that they can solve the problem they've just heard. Wrong!

DO NOT ATTEMPT TO SOLVE THE PROBLEM AT THIS POINT!

Here's why. Have you ever appreciated a friend who lets you unload a problem, only to become frustrated or angry when the friend tries to tell you how to solve it? Business has taught us to be ready with solutions. "Bring me solutions when you bring me problems" is yet another of those shopworn business clichés. People most often just want to unload, to talk about problems, to kick ideas around with someone they trust. When we have a problem, we want the solution to be ours as well. Remember my son's 89 in math class? He didn't want me to tell him how to get a 90. He wanted a hug.

Aspiring new rainmakers, who have had sales training, experience great difficulty when the easterly dialogue moves south. They want to present a solution, book the business, and move on.

Your greatest risk in an interview is that you'll turn into a sales rep as soon as you can visualize a solution!

Jumping in the executive's face with the solution this early in a relationship sounds something like this:

You're lucky that I came here today! Tah-dah! Looks like I can save your company. Most of our clients have this same problem. Look! We even have a brochure on this problem (you idiot!). We can fix this problem in a New York minute!

Ouch! Besides administering a blistering interpersonal blow, this hell-bent-to-solve-the-problem behavior will get you delegated downward to operations or purchasing people, who will analyze your solution and put it on their bid list. Jumping to solution conclusions will push you away from the executive and undermine your desire to become a Trusted Advisor. Following are two appropriate responses you can give to an executive who asks your opinion early in the relationship:

1. Start the solution phase by asking, "What have you done up to this point to solve this issue?" (Yes, ask another question.) This point is noted with an asterisk (*) on the compass between east and south. The question is important for several reasons: You'll learn if anyone else has been working on this issue—that is, if it's competitive. You'll learn more about the priority of the issue in the executive's mind (if the executive's done nothing to solve it, it may not be that important and you should go back to north and probe for another issue). You won't be inclined to suggest a solution that has already been tried. You'll learn more about the person, the human being with whom you are speaking, as your discussion continues—a crucial step on the Compass.

   The most important reason to ask what's been done so far to solve the issue is that the executive's answer will give you insight into how he or she thinks. People reveal volumes of information about themselves when they tell you how they approach solving problems. The right outcome here is to be able to determine whether the executive will accept help and also how much help might be appreciated.

2. Once you have gained appreciation for the executive's thought process, offer some ideas about your capability. *Introduce your solution ideas by asking more questions:*
   - "I couldn't help thinking about XWY Company as you were speaking. It opened up its customer order process on the Web so that customers can now check their own order status. How would something like that work here?"
   - "FedEx put communication devices in their trucks to make locating packages easier. Have you seen them, and how do you think that kind of idea would fit into your company?"

A rainmaker's task at south is to *brainstorm ideas*. It's *not to propose solutions!* Do you remember our telling you that getting an executive appointment isn't the hard part? The hard part is getting invited back for the second meeting. Offering a solution, especially a complex one, at this point in your first conversation could send the executive running for cover. Set the stage for a second conversation at this point. It's much better to continue a dialogue than to turn it into a sales pitch.

THE 80/20 RULE

You'll notice that within each of the easterly quadrants on the compass is "40%." This is a guideline that reminds you to ask and listen 80 percent of the time and talk less than 20 percent. When you combine the 19 percent in the next quadrant with the easterly 80 percent, the message is clear. It says:

> *Keep the focus on the client's issue, the client, and mutually brainstormed solution ideas for 99 percent of the dialogue. Talk about yourself, your products, and your company 1 percent!*

West

West is that portion of the dialogue in which you talk briefly about yourself and your capabilities. But once again this part should not dilute your focus on the customer. You have to find an appropriate way of closing this session without delivering a sermon about your virtues. The fact that you have survived to this point and are engaged in a dialogue should tell you that a sales pitch is not necessary. A productive interview that has followed the compass around the easterly side should conclude with comments that sound something like this:

> *Thank you for your time today. I really enjoyed our visit, and I especially appreciated your candor and your willingness to trust me with your issue about the _____. I wish I could solve it for you, but if it were that easy, you would have already solved it!*
>
> *I'd like to think about our conversation and also speak in confidence with some of my associates who may have seen this kind of issue. Then I'd like to come back and kick it around with you some more. Would you like to get together again next week, perhaps Tuesday?*

You have just solved your problem of getting the second appointment. We can't recall ever having an executive say no to a second appointment when an interview has followed the compass all the way to west. So confirm the time and date, say goodbye, and leave. Write down any notes you think are necessary as soon as you get in your car. Congratulations! You didn't give a presentation. You just facilitated your first customer executive meeting, and you're going back for more!

FOLLOW-UP

It's not time to celebrate just yet! Now you must ensure staying in your rainmaker role during your second visit. A natural inclination would be to return to your office, convene a meeting with sales and marketing folks, and write a proposal. The problem with that approach: *You don't have enough information.* Your impressions are based on a dialogue with one executive. You need more data to be sure that your initial solution idea is appropriate. Chances are that it's not!

Rather than writing a proposal, convene a small team of "experts" from your company who can listen to your description of your dialogue with the customer executive. Your experts might represent your sales, marketing, finance, product development, and manufacturing departments, or they might even include representatives from your alliance partners' organizations. It's important to get a mix of disciplines. The right solution for your customer may ultimately require product changes or special features, creative financing options, special shipping or warehousing, or any number of creative ideas that should be constructed up front. That will eliminate internal haggling and turf battles that are embarrassing and tedious. The initial invitees should represent areas within your business that match up with the information your customer gave you.

THE SECOND MEETING

We suggest that you invite one or two of your team members to accompany you to the second meeting for the following reasons:

- Bringing additional people enables you to introduce the size and breadth of your company.
- Bringing people who work at different levels within your organization enables you to begin to set up a Pyramid structure.
- Most important, this is an opportunity where mentoring can begin for some of your associates.

If you discover that one of your standard products will do the job before your second meeting, relax and remember that you want to bring more than an order back to your company. You are on a mission to develop a trusted relationship that signals a new approach to your customers, an approach that will give you *the relationship advantage.*

START THE JOURNEY

You are ready to begin the second meeting with your loosely constructed solution ideas firmly in mind. By now you are becoming comfortable with this new approach, but your team members haven't sat in on an interview, so caution them up front about the flow you want to establish in the meeting. Tell them to watch you, wait for your signal, and keep quiet until you ask for their ideas.

The reason for your admonitions is that after you adjourned your first interview last week, you went on to other businesses, customers, and issues. But your customer executive didn't. He kept thinking and processing your dialogue and is now ready to tell you all the things he wished he had told you but didn't. That means there are more data available for you to mine before you solve the problem. The original issue often grows in size with the addition of these new data.

Don't be surprised if your host has invited others to join the meeting. I can't tell you how many times we've heard executives say, for example, "I didn't get all of my facts exactly right last time, so I've invited the real experts here today to set us all straight." This is good because it presents the elements of the customer's Pyramid with which you can begin to match up. This happens all the time in your sales presentations as well, but your sales reps are too busy thinking about presenting their agenda to notice. They're also stifling the butterflies in their stomachs because they have to find a way to be interest*ing!* They also usually face the customer alone with little help or backup from their executive team. This is where the opportunity to build a relationship is squandered in countless sales presentations.

Where should you start the second meeting on the Compass?

Begin at north! Then go east!

Review your first interview, seek additional inputs, and give the new customer invitees a chance to add to the dialogue, thereby expanding the dialogue from one-on-one to several-on-several.

Start this second meeting by restating what you heard in the first meeting. The optimal introduction would be for your customer executive to restate the dialogue. Ask him what things might have been offered in error. Ask the others for their inputs. Ask them how they deal with the issues being considered from their positions in the organization (process questions). Ask what they've done to solve the problem in the past. Find out how they think, and brainstorm solution ideas with them. When they run out of ideas, have your teammates start to suggest your ideas through brainstorming. Keep prompting and don't fall into a presentation. That opportunity will come later.

It's OK to take notes in this second meeting as long as you are not the one doing it. Have one of your teammates take the notes for the whole group, and send copies to the customer attendees after the meeting adjourns.

If your customer is waiting for you alone and begins by asking you, "What have you got for me today?" or "Have you got this thing figured out yet?" you'll have to adjust slightly. In this case you should ask your teammates to wait for you in the lobby and maybe take one associate with you. You will know how to read this situation if you are paying attention to your customer's obvious agenda. If not—if you are too focused on your own agenda—you'll make the mistake of loading up your side of the conference table, which can make executives uncomfortable. No one likes to discuss confidential problems in front of an audience, so be sensitive in these cases and try a little empathy.

Once you follow the Compass with a customer or individual, never stop using it. Always start north, and then go east!

Once your associates have seen you following the Compass in a customer interview, insist that they begin using it in their daily meetings with their peers, whatever their level. This is how mentoring programs begin, customer by customer, one customer at a time.

Sam recalls how one of the managers he mentored at IBM adopted the Compass and became a lifelong practitioner of the process.

A C o m p a s s   " B l a c k   B e l t "

This good friend and successful IBM sales executive is a Compass "Black Belt" for both customer interviews and mentoring his colleagues. Tom was an IBM client rep when we met in the early 1990s at a consultative sales training workshop I was conducting as part of IBM's salesforce transformation initiative. A few weeks after the workshop, Tom called to ask if I would help him prepare a Compass for an upcoming customer meeting. Our coaching relationship continued and now, 12 years later, Tom is still a Compass practitioner.

I asked him recently what aspects of the Compass he finds most useful. His response: "The Compass is an extremely valuable tool for preparing for customer meetings. It works in all cases, but I have found it particularly helpful in planning for executive meetings, where time is limited. The Compass keeps me focused on asking strategic questions and listening actively, which leads to productive discussions about the customer's critical issues."

Over the past 12 years, Tom also developed a strong set of consulting and facilitation, or expediting, skills, both of which are critical to becoming a Trusted Advisor, working with a customer to address business issues and problems. Once consulting and facilitation skills are learned, practiced, and understood, they can be integrated into all customer interactions. Tom's ability to integrate consulting and facilitation skills into his sales behavior increased his confidence about collaborating with his customers to define and deliver high-impact solutions.

Tom's manager also acknowledged his accomplishments by indicating he'd love to replicate his capabilities and unique skills within the regional team. He asked Tom to find ways to help the other team members learn the Compass as well as develop consulting and facilitation capabilities, so they can use them to engage their customers more effectively.

PRESENTATION

It's appropriate to schedule a solution presentation only when you and the customer reach a mutual understanding of the problem to be solved. Be wary of the urge to return to your traditional sales methods at this juncture. That would be the easy course of action, especially if one of your standard products comprises most of the solution.

Can you imagine an end result more gratifying than seeing your customer's employees selling your product to their executives while you watch? That may sound outrageous, but it happens. We are suggesting that you involve the customer's team members in your presentation. Let them promote the problem statement and solution requirements. Then allow one of your highly trained sales reps to do what she does best: present product features and benefits, schedule installation events, and present financing information. Letting your reps do the presentation brings them in at the right level, uses their capabilities to the fullest extent, and—most important—keeps your role as rainmaker intact. You'll destroy all the personal credibility you have built up to this point if you revert to being a traditional sales rep. Turning your dialogue into a sales pitch will forever change the customer's perception of you from rainmaker back to sales presenter.

HOME RUN OR SINGLE?

Remember the information we offered earlier about hitting singles? If you wind up presenting a complex solution, and especially if the solution includes services that are wrapped around the product(s), then we suggest considering the singles' approach. You can do this by breaking your complex solution into phases for implementation. Present the first phase using an approach like the following:

Sounds like we're in agreement on the basic solution. Now it's time to talk about how best to implement it. We suggest keeping this team intact, at least through the first couple of phases. Phase One should encompass formalizing the problem statement, clearly defining the implementation plan and schedule, and selecting the first area of your business for imple-

mentation. I will stay involved from our company, and I'll not charge for my time. (This is the time to share risk as we pointed out earlier.) Mr. Executive, I'd like your assurance that you'll stay involved as well. It's important that the team stay just as it is for a while and that neither of us begins to delegate responsibilities until we develop a grooved swing around what we're doing. We'll be here every step of the way. We'd like your help getting our sales team positioned correctly with your purchasing and operations people. Can we get started next week?

Does this engagement method appeal to you? Does it strike a chord—help you recall the way you have seen rainmakers operate with you or your company when they have engaged? Your current job description doesn't require that you engage with your customers in this way. Surely, your company doesn't have a documented job description for any executive who leads customer executives through the Compass. In other words, you have always regarded this kind of activity to be the responsibility of others in your company, most likely your salesforce. Your executives have never led this kind of customer effort, and your salesforce has never experienced the level of artillery cover that this method would offer to them.

Assuming you want to try to do this, let's reiterate what countless rainmakers have confirmed to us about these situations so you'll know what to expect:

- *The solution, no matter how well defined it seems at the time, will change and grow.* Think back to the house-building example; people never know for sure everything they'll require when they start a complex project. Rainmakers find that the value of projects usually doubles when compared with the client's first budget.
- *Setting up a single is most likely the only way to keep the customer executive engaged.* If the effort is too big and complex, the executive won't want to commit an undetermined amount of time to it.
- *It is extremely important for your customer executive to see you and your team performing in the early stages,* and it's therefore extremely important that you *do* perform. Do what you promised. Do it on time or early. Once you get this far, you have passed the credibility test and trust is the next frontier.

TRY GOING BACKWARD

The Compass can also be used to illustrate the kinds of behaviors that keep many companies forever entombed in the status of vendor. Let's illustrate this point by working our previous situation backward. Look at the Compass again (on page 143). Let's start with a sales presentation. Let's go west!

This strategy presumes that no research has been done, and therefore no process questions have been considered or constructed. All you can do, given these conditions, is make a presentation and hope to connect with your audience in some way. The following scenario represents some of the presentations that I personally witnessed through the years at Cisco and IBM. We'll pick on Cisco a little bit here because its briefing process is more current. Here's how customer executives were greeted by their Cisco briefing hosts and hostesses who went west out of the gate:

> *Good morning, and welcome to Cisco. My name is ____ and I am responsible for our ____ department here at Cisco's headquarters. I've held this position for ____ months/years. I have also held the positions of ____ and ____. Prior to Cisco I worked at ____. By the way, do any of you know how we selected the name Cisco? Well, if you shorten San Francisco to just Cisco, you've got it! Here is a chart that shows our remarkable financial performance throughout the past decade. You'll notice that we've used the Golden Gate Bridge in the background, and you can see that our revenues and profits fit nicely on the upward curve of that cable span! At the stock market's opening this morning, our market cap sat at $250 billion, making us the number ____ company on the Nasdaq. I'd like to take a few minutes to show you how we view the industry, and I'll share some of our strategy and plans with you. [And on, and on, and on for about 50 charts!]*

See how different east and west are? To be fair, many people visited Cisco to find out more about the company, and it was a good idea to have a standard set of charts that every presenter could use to ensure consistency. The information we presented wasn't the problem. Rather, the positioning of the Cisco information at the front end of the meetings stifled customers' willingness to communicate at times. We were interest-*ing*, not interest*ed*. For example, when a presenter opened a monologue with "Our market cap is $250 billion," customers probably thought, "Ours isn't!"

> *Once you go west to start a meeting, you then naturally go south! When you go west, you're like a bomb looking for a target! You're fully armed, you're ready to detonate, and you're falling through space hoping to hit near an important point. Maybe you'll get lucky. But as the old saying goes, "Being close only counts in horseshoes—and grenades!"*

I vividly remember being invited to IBM's briefing center in Boca Raton, Florida, as an advisory board member for its PC business. Our hosts made us sit for hours on end, listening as presenter after presenter regaled us with information about their particular areas of responsibility. Never did they ask us to present anything about our business, plans, or strategy. These presentations always reminded me of a television interview with the famous singer/actress Diana Ross in which she talked incessantly about herself and her performances. When she finally ran out of gas, she turned to the interviewer and said, "Well that's enough about *me*. What did *you* think about *my* performances?"

Compaq approached its advisory board in an entirely different manner. About ten of us, all PC retail executives—Compaq's top channel partners—would convene in Houston. Ben Rosen, then chairman of Compaq, and Rod Canion, president, would preside over the meetings. The Compaq sales and marketing staff members waited together in another room. Rosen and Canion asked all of us to present our biggest business challenges, and they wrote our responses on flip charts. Then they asked the appropriate staff members to come in and strategize with us. Each Compaq staff department left the meetings with assignments on what needed to be fixed. The rate of follow-through was incredible. Know what? They rapidly began to eat IBM's PC market share for lunch!

What kind of customer meetings does your company conduct? What does your corporate culture dictate when customers are invited to your facilities? Here is a basic rule that puts a nice finish on this topic:

ONCE YOU'VE STARTED GOING WEST, YOU CAN'T REVERSE YOUR DIRECTION AND GO EAST.

It's physics! It's like gravity. Once you start down the slippery slope to the west, how can you possibly bring the conversation back to north? This is especially problematic if you don't have research data and haven't constructed any questions. You can only ask fake, tricky, shopworn questions and hope for a good result. If you're in this shape, how can you prompt a discussion about issues? How can you draw out the real person with whom you're speaking? How can you find out how they think? Going east or west will take you south, and each direction offers you the opportunity to put your agenda on the table.

The important consideration: How do you want your agenda to land on the table? The following questions deserve some reflection:

- Which direction would you like to go? What's stopping you?
- Which way would you like to be led if you were the customer? Which way is more pleasing?
- Which way offers the better chance to initiate a relationship?
- Which way better positions you to be a trusted advisor?

WHADDA YA GOT?

Here's an actual client interview that reinforced the preceding concepts for me. The following situation probably mirrors many of your own sales opportunities.

C l i e n t   I n t e r v i e w

I received a call one day from a CEO who was desperately seeking help for his business. Another executive had referred me to him. He was in a state of panic on the phone. He said that his company had been the market leader in an industry he had invented (his company remanufactured used integrated circuit components for computers), but they had lost their lead and were heading for the bottom. He wanted me to affirm that I could help him. I wanted to be truthful, and because I'd never met him, I couldn't give him that assurance.

(continued)

I finally said, "Look, I'm in Atlanta and you're in Phoenix. If you'll fly me out there and house me for a day at your expense, I'll waive my fees—and we'll see what we can do together." (Risk sharing)

I did some research, put together a couple of process questions, and flew to Phoenix two weeks later. He met me in his lobby at 7:00 AM the next morning to avoid creating any suspicions among members of his staff. We walked into his conference room, where I observed four other well-dressed gentlemen sitting at the table. They had obviously been there for a while, appeared alert, but didn't speak to me—not one word!

My host announced my arrival, told me to take the empty seat at the head of the table and explained, "These gentlemen are my board of directors. They're busy people—so we'll need to get right to work. OK?" What was I going to say? I hadn't even had time to sit down! I wondered in passing where they had found the coffee they were drinking.

As my posterior hit the chair, my host reiterated that we had to get right to work, and I assured him that I had received that message. He then looked me in the eye and said, "So tell us, Tom. Whadda ya got?"

Is that not a great example of an invitation to go west? I was dumbfounded and almost took the bait. But Sam Barcus's immortal words— "Go east!"—were ringing in my ears! The mood was set to my disadvantage and I had to reset it, or this was going to be a very short meeting.

I remember smiling and saying, "I'll tell you what I don't got! I don't got any coffee!" He quickly remedied that situation, and this activity seemed to relax him a bit. Then I continued, "Before I bore you with what I've got, I'd like to resolve something. Something caused you to call me and invite me out here. It sounded serious on the phone. So let me ask you—"Whadda you got?" (Risky? What did I have to lose?)

There was an incredible silence in the room! No one spoke; in the old days this is where we would've reached for a cigarette. I was determined not to speak first. After about 30 seconds—which seemed like 30 minutes—one of the board members looked in my direction and said, "Whadda we got? You want to know whadda we got?" I gratefully shook my head up and down, and he said, "A mess! That's what we got! A mess!" I asked if he could be more specific, and he explained that the company didn't have any business discipline. He said they lacked systems and controls—that they couldn't even tie their sales orders to their inventory, and customers were going elsewhere for service.

Then another board member jumped in and corrected the first by telling me that their big problem was lack of control in hiring. As he spoke, I went to the white board and began writing down their main points. When the board was full, I asked for a flip chart stand and paper. They talked, I wrote. Occasionally I stopped the conversation and suggested they stay focused on a particular point.

They brought in sandwiches at noon. At about 3:00 PM I announced that I had to leave for my flight. The CEO surmised that this had been the best meeting they had ever had as a team—and he wanted to pay me for my time. I protested that we had made a different agreement, but he insisted. I told him what my daily rate was, and he departed to draw a check for me. I asked the board members (whom I still hadn't met—didn't know their names) for permission to take the flip charts with me. As I was rolling them up, one of the gentlemen said, "What in the hell did you do here today?" When I replied that they had done the heavy lifting, that all I'd done was observe, he smiled and said, "I know. That's what's behind my question. We did the work, but we're paying you!"

I returned to Atlanta that night with a compendium of their issues. The biggest one I had was determining which to attack first. Although this meeting was clearly unique, it provokes many thoughts. Grab your Compass diagram and think through this for a moment:

- How different would the outcome have been if I had answered the "Whadda ya got" question first?
- Where would the meeting have gone if I had started talking about myself, some of my success stories, or my methods?

Consider this meeting in the context of a sales call. Were I a sales rep I probably would have told my story first. I would have gone west! As I overwhelmed them with my references, they would undoubtedly have asked me questions about fees and expenses—"What did they pay for that?" The meeting would have lasted as long as I had information to present. They probably would have thanked me for coming, and if they were impressed would have asked me for brochures, a fee schedule, and references.

But here's the worst part of this scenario. Had I been working for a corporation, I would have jumped on the plane, whipped out my laptop, and begun entering data about that company into my forecast. I would have told CRM that I needed at least six months to develop the business. But I also would have stated—correctly—that I had met at the highest executive level. I'd met with the CEO and the whole board of directors! But I'd still be dumb as a stone regarding that company's issues.

FINAL THOUGHT

A final thought: Be careful with the context statements that start your process questions. They can become tedious and self-focused if you don't monitor them carefully. Even the best-constructed question can pose a momentary tug-of-war at the top of the Compass if the customer asks you a question first. If that happens, and it will, answer the question thoroughly but quickly, and then follow with your question again. If you fail to do this, you'll go to the west! Don't be surprised if this tug-of-war occurs two or three times at the start of your meetings. You just have to read what's going on and persevere. Remember, someone's going to do the majority of the talking and someone's going to do most of the listening. Keep your goal in mind and don't relinquish your right to be interest*ed*.

The Compass has been the most appreciated and referenced part of our lives for the past decade—it is Sam's greatest invention! People who participated with us in sessions from all over the globe run into us at trade shows and other events and thank us for introducing them to this simple metaphor for success. We hope that when we meet you, you'll say, "Hey Sam and Tom, I'm going east!"

SUMMARY

We know that no two companies will implement the Compass in exactly the same way. Hybrids are fine, but the key is to get started. Try it a sufficient number of times until you are able to create a personal version of the Compass that works for you. If you help your executive team understand how important its personal accountability is in building trusted relationships with customers, you've moved the ball a long way down the field. The critical elements at the beginning are these:

- Executive and top management involvement
- Team involvement for those whom you want to mentor in your new process
- A strong belief that executing the Compass makes your job as "vendor" easier and more productive

Indeed, this strong belief makes you more than a vendor. It can make you a Trusted Advisor.

Part Three

A PATH
TO SUCCESS

12

DIAGNOSE
AND PRESCRIBE

Early on we characterized rainmak-
ers as problem solvers. Problem solving requires an interesting mix of
facilitation skills, processes, and interpersonal skills. The purpose of this
chapter is to provide you—our new rainmakers—a short course in the
art of solving problems.

In our chapter on the Compass we discussed the wisdom of breaking down customer opportunities into small pieces in order to enable the
relationship wheels to start rolling forward when rainmakers engage on
a project following their executive interviews. Rainmakers use problem-
solving techniques like the ones we are about to reveal in every client engagement, from the initial team meetings to the meetings at the end of
projects. This problem-solving model is so well documented that a rainmaker's people can be taught easily to use it by watching their mentors
execute meetings. For this reason, we think you will be able to adopt this
technique rather easily as well. You might want to try using it to work
through an internal issue with your own staff members first before using
it to facilitate customer meetings.

THE TEAM MEETING

A diagnostic problem-solving meeting should be held in a quiet, out-of-the-way setting to make it easy for all of the participants to keep their focus. The meeting works best when conducted in a small group—no more than ten participants—with an erasable whiteboard and blank flip charts available. The attendees should include the sponsoring customer executive, managers from the executive's team, and staff members from the rainmaker's firm who match up appropriately with the customer's people. Ideally, all participants observed a Compass interview session where they were mentored in the use of these structured approaches to solving problems prior to the meeting.

The customer executive who brought up the issue in the Compass interview should start the meeting with a personal explanation of the issue to be resolved. Executives, when faced with explaining an issue to their team members, typically display an intuitive feel that "something is wrong." They often find it difficult to articulate their concern as clearly as they did when the rainmaker was leading them with good questions in the interview. So be patient and don't try to speak for the executive. Remember, the executive must own the problem and its solution—not you!

Although Compass interviews help zero in on problems, they really serve only to get the process rolling. The process we're about to describe provides a more comprehensive method to help define and articulate what the real problems and their root causes may be. Don't be surprised if your customer executive begins with a statement like this:

> *I've been reviewing our past three quarters, and we've lost some efficiency somewhere between our customer orders and the shipping process at our warehouse. The departments involved don't seem to be singing from the same sheet of music, and I'll be damned if I can figure out the reason. We've lost five points of margin, and customer satisfaction has dropped as well. I think the way we set goals around here may have something to do with this problem.*

What can you do with a statement like that? It's vague, but it also includes several interesting clues for an alert problem-solving team to explore. The executive knows there is a communication glitch somewhere in the logistics process; it's costing about five points of gross margin; and the "sheet of music" reference suggests that departmental goals and objectives conflict with each other.

Both causes and effects are apparent in the executive's statement. The "causes" are poor communication and conflicting goals and objectives. The "effects" are loss of profit margin and low customer satisfaction. The rainmaker's job—yours if you're up to it—is to assist the team through an exercise that enables them to discover what specific problems and issues are causing the executive's problem. *The key point to remember is to work on the causes, not the effects. If the causes are fixed, the effects will change.*

Given a vague statement like this, a rainmaker's value is established when the executive sees vague thoughts turned into a clear, concise problem statement. The executive's participation in the meeting is essential, because the executive must ultimately own the problem and its solution as well as own the feeling of accomplishment that comes with solving a "big one."

CONSTRUCT THE DESIRED OUTCOME

Look now at the "Problem-Solving Template" in Figure 12.1. The rainmaker must first introduce the concept of a *desired outcome*. The facil-

FIGURE 12.1 *The Problem-Solving Template*

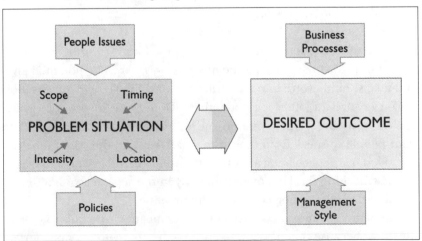

itator starts by acknowledging the ambiguity in the executive's problem statement and then starts the process by asking a question like this:

> *If things in this area were working correctly, what would be different and better than what you see today? What would the ideal situation look like?*

The facilitator is really asking, "What outcome(s) would you like to see?" Process and content questions like this one should be used appropriately during the discussion to keep the executive's information flow going, just as we used them in the interview. The executive will begin to open up to the questions *if* the facilitator and team members allow the executive to answer without argument or needless interruption. You have to keep close watch on this situation because a client's staff members will often see these sessions as opportunities to impress the boss. We don't need any of that behavior, so you may have to nip it in the bud at the first occurrence by establishing a team rule: "one speaker at a time."

As the executive warms to the environment, you (you are now the facilitator) can sharpen your questions and become more specific. You have to listen very carefully to each statement the executive makes so that your content and process questions keep the discussion on course. You can be more specific by asking questions such as:

> *If the distribution center's employees coordinated their activities properly with the manufacturing and marketing staffs, how would the workflow and results differ from those you see today?*

Responses to process questions like these always prompt additional questions if you are managing the meeting correctly. The potential give-and-take should evolve into a very intense and interesting conversation as you involve the other team members. Doing that is your job, which you do by asking, "Which one of you has expertise on this point?" You want people to speak from their own expertise, and they should be discouraged from speculating about another team member's area of expertise. Establishing this kind of control early in the session avoids allowing any single person to hog control of the meeting.

Remaining interested is the correct demeanor to exhibit in these meetings because the dialogue turns on your ability to ask appropriate questions, listen to responses, and queue up additional questions based on the team members' responses.

The answers to all questions should be written on the whiteboard or flip chart pages. Brainstorming like this, when properly facilitated, produces a thorough list of things that could be different and improvements that could change the status quo. Be sure to write all of the answers on the board or on flip charts. Don't try to judge their impact at this point; that comes later.

The discussion will eventually dissolve into topics of minor or no impact. You need to watch when this begins to happen to ensure that your meeting doesn't turn into a "gripe session." When you sense that the conversation has taken this turn, help the participants prioritize their written answers based on which ones will have the greatest impact (top) to the least impact (bottom). Numerical rankings and alphabetical schemes (A, B, C) work fine; the group should decide which option to use.

Once the outcome statements have been prioritized, you have paved the way for creation of a simple, coherent statement of the *desired outcome*. The statement may be several short sentences, or it may be one simple idea expressed in one sentence. You are enabling real diagnosis here, and executives become engaged when they see their ambiguous statements emerging into actionable sentences. Creating a statement of the desired outcome has an additional benefit for the team; it gives them a more concrete sense of purpose and a higher purpose to pursue.

Creating the *desired outcome statement* can be greatly enhanced by keeping the team focused on using what we call *evaluation criteria,* which help the team think through the results to be achieved by the outcome. These criteria can be used to compare the relative benefits of the various desired outcome ideas and help determine the final choice. The following questions are good ones to use when trying to identify evaluation criteria. Keep in mind that criteria should be stated in a way that identifies the specific end results to be achieved:

- What would the ideal outcome achieve?
- What would the ideal outcome avoid?
- What would the ideal outcome preserve?
- What are the constraints for this decision (time, money, resources, people)?
- Based on your experience, what other criteria should be considered?

Defining the desired outcome is an extremely important step in the process. In fact, the entire success of your team's efforts hinges on your ability to accomplish this step correctly and efficiently; and it may take more than one meeting. There are no shortcuts to this step. Does the importance of defining what your customer wants by using a process like this explain why prepackaged solutions turn executives off when they are presented at the beginning of a dialogue?

BUILD THE PROBLEM SITUATION

In the next step, defining the *problem situation,* your task is to enable the team to determine what specific problems exist that make the desired outcome difficult to achieve. Although the executive mentioned a few problems in his opening statement, the team will not only clarify those problems but will give you more. The reason you want to define the problem situation immediately after you have defined the desired outcome is that adhering to this sequence puts the executive's concerns into a context where the team can actually deal with them. The major task for the team to accomplish in this step is to combine all of their problem statements into one succinct problem statement: the Problem Situation Statement.

The best way to ensure clarity of thought and expression at this point in the meeting is to have the team members state their thoughts in complete sentences. For example, instead of accepting a *problem statement* such as "Warehouse Communications," you can continue to work that statement by asking, "What elements of the warehouse communications need improvement? What's really wrong there?" The goal is to reach agreement on what the *root cause* is of any problem that is suggested in the dialogue. Stating the problem clearly is of primary importance in accomplishing that goal.

Rather than simply accepting a problem statement like "Warehouse Communications," use the kernel of that thought to create a clearer statement such as this: "People in the warehouse are unaware of how much the sales department relies on their timely reporting of outages." This clearer terminology serves the team better than a two-word phrase as time goes by in the session. People tend to forget somewhere between 50 and 80 percent of the details of a discussion after a few days. Therefore, it's best to write down any and all ideas in complete sentences so that the meaning won't be unclear or become challenged later on in the exercise.

In our graphic illustration of the Problem-Solving Template (Figure 12.1), you'll see four ways exist to qualify each problem statement. Once all of the team's contributions to the problem statement question have been recorded on charts, you will then lead a detailed discussion about each individual recorded response. The four qualifiers to be tested against each statement are scope, timing, intensity, and location. Following are the definitions of these four qualifiers:

1. *Scope.* Consider the size and breadth of the problem. How far does it extend throughout the business? Is it internally generated and therefore within management's control or is it externally caused by industry, economic, or other factors?
2. *Timing.* Consider when and how often the problem occurs: monthly, quarterly, daily. Be sensitive to interest rate changes and other cyclical market occurrences.
3. *Intensity.* Consider how strongly the issue is felt, who feels it, and how the degree of intensity is exhibited.
4. *Location.* Consider where the problem presents itself. Is it widespread or confined to an office or department; is it present within the walls of the company only or also present in external locations?

WRITE A CLEAR STATEMENT

It is important to have the executive, who articulated the problem, participate in the creation of this assignment or even lead the discussion if the executive so desires. All of the discussion and group documentation up to this point should make it fairly easy to construct a clear, concise Problem Situation Statement. The statement should be tight and as short as possible, and at the end the executive should say, "Yeah, that gets it. That's what I meant to say."

When constructing a Problem Situation Statement, it may be helpful to keep these things in mind:

• Answer the scope, timing, intensity, and location questions with *facts.* Don't guess or accept hearsay.

- Try to avoid forcing information into the statement. Just consider each statement to the best of your ability and then move on.
- Team members may question the meaning of certain ideas. Circle those facts whose interpretation is in question on the charts using red or some other highly visible color for emphasis. Gain agreement on the acceptable interpretation and then proceed to the next item. You need only verify interpretations that turn out to be critical to your analysis.
- All four of the qualifiers might not apply to each and every problem. If a qualifier does not help to identify relevant information, skip it.
- Help the team to always be specific in every definition.
- Stay on task. Answer the questions for this aspect of the session, and don't focus on other aspects of the problem-solving process until the appropriate time.

Your Problem Situation Statement for this sample exercise should read something like this:

> *The compensation and recognition policies in the warehouse differ from those used in accounting, finance, sales, and marketing, which causes most departments to have poor communication with the warehouse. This in turn induces us to do a poor job of fulfilling customer orders on the dates we have promised. Sales is therefore discounting our prices to these customers in order to retain their business, which in turn is killing profits.*

More Qualifiers to Consider

The kind of statement above will engage the executive who started the discussion, but we're not yet finished with this portion of the session. Four additional ways to qualify your problem statements are spread around the exterior of the diagram in Figure 12.1. The first four qualifiers we used in our definition of the problem dealt with mostly *quantitative* issues. The next four items are more *qualitative,* and they require that you conduct another level of discussion to further clarify the problem.

The importance of using these additional four qualitative qualifiers will become obvious in the next steps when you help your team define the obstacles. Running the team's diagnostic work against these final qualifiers makes everyone feel comfortable that the problem is defined as well as that this group can solve it. Quick definitions for these four final items follow:

1. *People issues.* Consider any and all personnel issues that occur anywhere in the organization that may impact the problem. Examples would include voluntary resignations; training programs; skills deficiencies; critical job vacancies, especially in management or specialty areas; and newly acquired divisions.

2. *Policies.* Are there written or unwritten policies in the management process that may cause or impact the problem? Examples might be mandating vacations during critical business cycles; inflexible financial terms; product return policies; charitable contributions; community involvement; and warranty administration.

3. *Business processes or procedures.* Are there processes and procedures that were created, perhaps in total quality management (TQM), incentive stock option (ISO), or other corporate initiatives, that might cause or have an impact on this problem? Many companies became process-bound in the 1990s as U.S. companies tried to install Japanese processes. These processes were often not implemented in response to specific problems.

4. *Management style.* This term, which rainmakers use to define the way a management team approaches and solves problems, represents the combined personality of the management team. Style expresses how a management team reflects and executes the company's goals and objectives. It answers the question, "Does management walk the talk?" Some companies have a bureaucratic style, often hidden within a hierarchy, making it hard to get things done. Others lack leadership and mandatory processes and procedures, leaving employees in the dark as to how best to get things done. Some companies demand and reward long hours, whereas others are flexible about time and allow workers to work from their home. Regardless of style, this point usually results in a long and profitable discussion.

Perhaps you remember seeing this famous quotation uttered by the little cartoon character Pogo: "We have met the enemy, and it is us!"

When you assist your client's team members by creating a Problem Situation Statement, you'll find the members make an important discovery. This kind of problem definition, or discovery, paired with your group discussions, enables top-level managers and executives to see how they might be "the enemy." A problem-solving exercise opens their eyes to the things they do, individually or as a team, that cause problems.

DEFINE THE OBSTACLES

Once the team agrees on the *desired outcome* and on a succinct Problem Situation Statement, the next task is to probe to find out what barriers impede achieving what the team wants. Some of the best corporate plans we've seen are merely documented recaps of the actions that can be taken to overturn the obstacles that stand in the way of achieving a desired outcome. Think about this:

> *If you know what you want—and know what's keeping you from getting it—then figuring how to get it solves the problem.*

You will lead another discussion, this time asking team members to articulate the obstacles they see standing in the way of achieving the desired outcome. You'll notice their tendency to restate some of the problem statements you collected in the last step. One way to elicit additional responses here is to ask the following kinds of questions:

- What could we change to get past this obstacle?
- Who can best change it?
- What will keep us from changing it? What's in the way?

Group brainstorming about the obstacles usually yields yet another list of answers. Keep the following in mind when brainstorming potential obstacles:

- *Keep it simple.* Simple explanations should be powerful enough to explain the gaps.
- *Tell the team to be as specific as possible.* Clearly state how each one of the obstacles is blocking the desired outcome. Remember to use complete sentences wherever possible

- *Try not to evaluate.* List everyone's ideas. Facilitators should not allow team members to judge each other's inputs and ideas. In brainstorming, no idea is a bad idea.
- *Don't let team members assume anything.* Look for proof of every obstacle that is volunteered by team members.

Experience has shown that qualifying obstacles this way enables a team to see the real ones and makes it easy to discard those of minor consequence. It brings clarity to ambiguous statements, such as the executive's vague problem statement we used to begin this chapter. But the greatest benefit is that defining the *desired outcome, problem situation,* and *qualified obstacles* defines the issue(s) with such clarity that practically any group can resolve it.

SOLUTION

Would you believe that problems sometimes solve themselves by this point in a team exercise? We have seen hundreds of problem-solving meetings in which the dialogue alone created such a clear understanding among the team members that they were able to solve the issue on the spot!

When you facilitate a dialogue like this, you'll immediately sense how the team's interchange co-opts all the members to get onto the same "sheet of music." Sometimes problems get solved as soon as the responsible parties are permitted to see them in detail. In other cases, however, the solution is not so obvious. In those cases the team's next step is to brainstorm solution ideas and create action steps that the team believes can overcome the obstacles it has defined.

The facilitator can be very helpful at keeping the team on task in this final phase of the session. Once the obstacles have been prioritized, the facilitator should lead the group through them one-by-one, making basic decisions on the following elements for each:

- What needs to be done to overcome this obstacle?
- Who can best lead this effort?
- What are the things to be done (list)?
- When will they be done?

- What interdependencies exist? Who else must help with this step?
- If the interdependencies create another obstacle, return to the basic exercise and put them into the mix.

The list of actions that the group agrees will overcome all of the obstacles will become the team's plan to resolve the problem situation. Your output from the session should be a master list of these actions, sorted two ways for each committed action—first, by the action's due date; second, by the person responsible for handling it. Each participant should be given the master list with due dates and individual responsibilities along with any interdependencies that require participants to work with others.

Following is an example of documentation that might have resulted from a session in which a management team was dealing with its ability to adopt *the relationship advantage:*

1. *Desired outcome.* We want to develop deeper, trusted relationships with our current customers. *Deeper* and *trusted* will be measured by the amount of involvement that we are invited to have with our customers' management teams' issues and problems.
2. *Problem situation.* The main problems that keep us from having the outcome we desire are these:
   - Our sales process doesn't involve executives and top managers.
   - Executives and top managers don't have time to be accountable for customer relationships.
   - Sales reps are paid on the basis of their ability to control accounts, and they don't want assistance from executives and top managers.
   - Our executives and top managers are measured on the basis of financial and operational performance, so they have no incentive to become involved in customer relationships.
   - Our executives and top managers don't have rainmaker experience, and it's not clear that they would allow themselves to be trained, especially if they might become embarrassed in front of their employees!
3. *Location, timing, scope, and intensity.* Our obstacles are not affected by timing or location issues:
   - The *scope* of obstacles is widespread, especially at the very top of our organization. The effect of the economic downturn is

that everybody is busy; suggesting that executives and top managers add customer accountability would have a widespread negative effect on them.

- The *intensity* of the sales reps' feelings about sharing accountability is deep, because reps perceive their pay could suffer if executives and top managers bungle the reps' accounts.

4. *Additional considerations:*

- The only business process issue is our deeply entrenched CRM system that requires everybody to play a role in customer responsibility. According to CRM, executives and top managers are the review point for sales reps' inputs, and they perform the data analysis that drives this process.
- Our greatest people issue is the inexperience of our top managers as it relates to customer relationship accountability. Most managers are either financial or technical/engineering people who have had limited exposure to customers during their careers.
- There are no policies that would keep us from implementing a Pyramid with our customers other than CRM-based practices that have become almost de facto policies.
- Our greatest issue is with our management style, because we have always recognized and applauded delegation. Turning executives and top managers into rainmakers flies in the face of our culture.

5. *Problem statement.* "Our desire to create deep, trusted relationships with our customers is hampered by our culture and many of our management practices. Our executives and top managers are taught to delegate; they are not measured or paid on the basis of their ability to affect customer relationships; they are bound to a CRM requirement to review and analyze data instead of creating the data; they expect our sales reps, all of whom are junior level and lack experience with rainmaking, to carry the ball with customer relationships. As a result, our sales reps resent executive intrusion into their accounts and feel that kind of assistance is not helpful. In addition to our culture, our goal and objective-setting methods along with our compensation scheme do not encourage our executives and top managers to get involved in customer relationships. Finally, we question our executives' and

Q *u i z*

See if this short quiz helps reinforce the ideas in this chapter.

1. *What is the first step in a problem definition exercise?*

2. *What are the two elements that make up a Problem Situation Statement?*

3. *Name the four primary, quantitative qualifiers for a problem situation.*

4. *Name the four qualitative qualifiers.*

5. *Why do rainmakers from consulting firms conduct problem definition meetings personally? Why don't they delegate the meetings to their junior employees?*

6. *What are the major benefits of leading customers through problem definition sessions?*

top managers' abilities to act in rainmaking roles as they have no practical experience doing so."

This Problem Situation Statement is ready for a solution. Can you see why it is so important to have an executive sponsor involved when you're creating a statement like this? Put differently, can you imagine how this statement would appear to most executive management teams if it were presented by a bunch of staff people who work at lower organizational levels? It would be disastrous, because it would look like a scathing criticism instead of a constructive idea, full of promise, for the organization's future.

A RAINMAKER'S VALUE

An objective outsider, working with your president, would be able to commiserate, share thoughts and experiences, and take a respectable shot at formulating a palatable solution. Can't you do the same for your top executives? Try engaging a meeting like this with those executives before you experiment with customers. The problem we chose for the preceding example—sales accountability—prompted us to write this book.

A suggestion to executives that they change their culture usually falls on deaf ears or makes them defensive. They will engage more if they collaborate on the definition of the issue and its solution. These are the kinds of issues that drive executives to find Trusted Advisors. Do you think your top executives would appreciate knowing they have someone on board who can lead them through a process like this? Are you willing and able to be that person? Why not practice on the sales accountability issue?

SUMMARY

The problem-solving process we've just described enables a team to clearly define a problem by clarifying what is desired and identifying what is obstructing its ability to achieve what it wants. Rainmakers accept personal accountability for facilitating these sessions so they can stay close to their client executives, thus ensuring their satisfaction.

This process also allows rainmakers to simultaneously mentor a client's team and their own people in the fine points of facilitation and problem solving. You will become a teacher and coach to your team and to the client executive. Your goal should always be to transfer these problem-solving and facilitation skills to the team members. The team members should be able to replicate the process for other problems once you have led them through the process.

Rainmakers contend the most important benefit that accrues from conducting a problem-solving session is its allowing them to spend many hours in a room with their key client executives, focusing on that client and his or her problem. This defines the parameters of a relationship in which the rainmaker can become a Trusted Advisor to the client executive.

If you invest the time to focus on a customer's issues and bring substantive value to the table, the customer will probably buy your product. The alternative is to wait for a consultant to define the customer's issues and hope to be selected when the product needs are defined. You may feel frustrated because you can't visualize yourself conducting an exercise like this right away. A realistic compromise may be to join a team exercise that is being conducted by a rainmaker for your customer. If you find during an interview that another rainmaker is currently facilitating a problem-solving session, it's not out of bounds to ask the executive to include you as another team member. Your odds for success increase when the customer executive begins to realize that you have his or her best interest at heart.

Why not visualize as a desired outcome for your company the creation of a new culture filled with rainmakers who are Trusted Advisors to your most important customers? It's all right there in front of you.

You *can* develop *the relationship advantage!*

13

DON'T BID
IF YOU CAN SELL

It's time to turn the spotlight on some of the traditional business practices that often block a management team from becoming Trusted Advisors to their customers. Reflect on your own customer-oriented business practices as you read these next few pages. Does your culture encourage your salesforce to look for opportunities to bid your products? Have you installed electronic systems to replace your human touch with customers? Does your management team seem bogged down in data analysis? Read on!

PROACTIVE OR REACTIVE:
DON'T BID IF YOU CAN SELL

We understand that you can't reorganize your whole business into a Pyramid. But you can realize some of a Pyramid's benefits if you'll think outside the box, employing some of the principles that define this organizational structure. What are some things you could do to motivate your top executives and managers to assume more personal accountability for customer relationships? Have you ever tried? If you are a top executive, would you consider becoming more accountable for some of your company's key customer relationships? We are talking about true accountability as opposed to making infrequent courtesy calls on your customers.

If you are *the* top executive, you could simply mandate a change for all executives who report to you. If you are one of your company's top managers, you may not have to wait for the mandate. You could implement a few test cases by matching yourself up with some of your customers' executives. You can bring your CEO or president on board after you demonstrate positive results from your experiment. Such an approach will reduce your personal risk while you build up your confidence. It will take time to achieve positive results, but it could be well worth the effort. We're certain that your sales reps would appreciate some "artillery cover" from their generals and colonels.

Often you don't hear about the ideas that are being developed in your customers' process teams until your daily contact asks you to submit your pricing information and product specifications to his or her bid committee so it can analyze you. This kind of analysis is based on your pricing, but your delivery schedules and product support may be important factors as well. This is a perfect segue to our next topic: bidding versus selling.

When a rainmaker's team diagnoses issues for your customers that result in orders for your products, it is often conducting the sell phase for your products in our marketing life cycle. At sell time, someone has to help a customer understand how a new idea or product can address a need; but at this early stage, the need is usually not well defined. No products will be sold until the customer, under the influence of a rainmaker, can see the alignment of his or her need with your product. *A product order transaction will not take place until the need for it is defined.* Defining needs in this way is what we referred to earlier as diagnostic work. Investing the time to manage all of these front-end elements of a customer's procurement cycle, including diagnosing issues and prescribing a solution, is what a rainmaker regards as *selling*.

When your sales reps submit product specifications and pricing in response to a request for information (ROI) or a request for pricing (RFP), they are not selling. They are *bidding*. Bids occur only when a customer understands what he needs, and then all he requires to move forward is information about price, delivery, support, financial terms, and customer references. Bid responses are *fulfill* activities at the bottom of the Value

Staircase and belong on the far right side of our Marketing Life Cycle. The customer's focus in bids is on *price,* not value.

Sell activity is at the opposite end of the customer's value spectrum. It takes place on the far left side of the Marketing Life Cycle where customers are focused on *value,* not price. The potential profit is higher when you *sell* because the customer perceives that he needs you to do more than bid your price. He needs your knowledge and expertise, and he places a high value on these things. Selling is not like a bid situation, where much of the customer's effort is comparative in nature—comparing your product with a similar offering from another.

> *When bidding, the highest value work has already been done. The customer knows he needs something. He just needs to get it in the most cost-effective manner possible.*

It may help to think of this distinction as follows: Selling is a *proactive activity* that allows you to take the initiative; bidding is a *reactive activity* because someone else has already taken the initiative to analyze the situation. All you can do in a bid is react to the analysis.

Some sales executives we work with refuse to respond to bids because they feel they can't add value to a situation in which they know the profit margin opportunity has been severely reduced. They also bemoan the way bidding creates a perception with their customers that they are reactive, that they are only adept at fulfilling orders. Behaving more like a rainmaker is the best way to get out of that trap!

Once customers acknowledge to themselves that yours is a reactive company, it's almost impossible to change that perception. How can you show customers on Monday that you specialize in responding to bids and on Tuesday convince them that you have the requisite experience to help them diagnose business problems? Customers' perceptions of your reactivity account for much of the frustration your sales reps feel when you send them to training classes that promise to teach them how to call on executives. It's like asking them to beat their heads against the wall!

We acknowledged earlier that there's a proper place for FBR and FFF sales calls. A bid situation is that place. Bid situations are almost always competitive; sales reps have to fight for their life as soon as they can get in front of the bid-letting customer, so they are forced to conduct monologues, present their product's features, recite the product's benefits, and push the customer into a positive reaction to their pitches. They soon discover that customers don't care about building trusted relationships when they are soliciting bids.

Let's go back to the proactive side for a moment. We *do* acknowledge that it is often necessary to respond to bids; however, this bidding tradition started years ago isn't important—it's real. We *do not* acknowledge that it's ever necessary to act as though you're bidding if the customer hasn't demanded you do so. If you have an opportunity to *sell,* why not take advantage of it? Your ability to grow and prosper may depend on the degree to which you can push yourself up on the Value Staircase. You may not be able to move all the way to the far left of the marketing life cycle with the professional rainmakers. But we challenge you to understand how far to the left you *can* move if you adopt some of the rainmaker attributes we've presented in this book.

EARLY BIDDING CASE STUDY

We have seen many companies fall into an interesting trap by encouraging their sales reps to *bid* their innovative products when they could *sell* them. These products are often so new that no competitive offerings exist in the marketplace. A company we know very well motivates its sales reps to push new products through the same process they use to move their best-selling commodities.

From a credibility standpoint, this company is frequently recognized in the trade press as a model of efficiency among all new economy companies. It touts its ability to hit sales forecasts and has backed up its boasting with solid performance. A large measure of its success can be attributed to its aggressive salesforce that is constantly under management's microscope. Sales reps and managers are measured on a daily, weekly, monthly, quarterly, and annual basis made possible by excellent computer systems and applications that allow executives in all areas of the business to know the status of all sales orders whenever they choose to tap into the systems to check on progress.

This supplier also books most of its business through third-party channel partners that resell its product lines to the ultimate end user. These channel partners sell to their own customers, and they also fulfill orders that are uncovered by the supplier's aggressive sales reps. The channel partners book the business, order the products from the supplier, install and maintain the products, and carry the financial exposure by collecting all monies owed from the end users.

A handful of these channel partners are distributors that specialize in stocking large quantities of commodity products that they buy from many different technology companies. Distributors sell to other channel partners and measure their success by the ability to provide immediate delivery at an acceptable price when they have the desired items in stock. The benefit provided to the marketplace is therefore referred to as Time–Place–Price. Thinking back to our marketing life cycle, this kind of business—a distributorship—would be categorized as *fulfill*. Distributors work on very low margins and rely on high volumes of product orders for their survival. New products that have not built any market momentum are therefore of little interest to them.

The largest component of the channel is made up of companies called *value-added resellers,* or VARs, that create solutions by integrating products and services from a number of suppliers. A directory of VARs would include IBM, NCR, Siemens, Alcatel, phone system carriers, major technology consulting firms, systems integrators, and thousands of regional and local technology providers.

To make money, VARs package products with unique value-based services, such as installation planning, product training, programming, and other support services. The services would be considered *manage* activities and therefore provide VARs with relatively higher profits than they would achieve by merely selling commodity products alone.

The problem: To sustain incredibly high growth rates during the technology boom of the 1990s (measured in double digits, quarter over quarter), this supplier had to push its salesforce extremely hard for each and every order every day. This created a perception among the salesforce that the sales reps had little or no time available for investing in planning, analysis, or any other *manage* activity. The reps therefore began to *bid* every product in their portfolio—that is, reps proposed discounted prices to their customers as their opening offer. They often proposed deep discounts when they were the first supplier in the customers' doors, and there were no other competitors in the potential deals. Once an opportunity was identified and the reps had created a discounted price expectation, VARs were then invited to book the business.

As we mentioned, VARs make their profit only when they add their services to a product sale. But the particular supplier's sales reps we're discussing created an expectation with customers that the VAR's services would also be discounted or provided free of charge. This represented a win-lose approach whereby the VARs lost profit but the supplier still got the sale. The VARs wound up taking the financial hit when this supplier's products were commoditized, but the supplier held his profit margin by holding the price to the resellers constant. The VARs found this practice especially painful when they were asked to offer deep discounts on a whole package that included their value-added services. Entire solution offerings were commodotized.

You would think that this sales practice would have been executed only for commodity products, but the supplier's brand-new, innovative products were also offered at commodity discount prices. The supplier's sales reps said:

> *Customers buy our mature products at discounted prices, so they expect the same discounts on new products. It takes too long to retrain customers to expect lesser discounts on new products, so we just go with what we know.*

This behavior frustrated the VARs. Loyalty to suppliers is largely determined by the degree to which the suppliers support their VARs ability to make higher profits when new products come along.

We spent more than three years educating the top managers of these VARs about the Pyramid and about selling from a value-based position. But they were constantly critical of this particular supplier because the VARs perceived they were being asked to place a higher value on the supplier's innovation than the supplier placed on it!

Putting the financial damage that was done to the VARs aside for a moment, it was the supplier that ultimately suffered the biggest negative impact, because *the practice of offering every product at a deep discount stripped margin dollars from new products, causing them to spiral down into commodity status much faster than was necessary.* Recall Kenny Rogers singing these lyrics in a famous song about a gambler: "You've got to know when to hold them, know when to fold them." We think the following modification to Rogers's lyrics works well in this discussion: "You've got to know when to *sell* them, know when to *bid* them!"

Sales Relationships

Another issue buried in this scenario is even more pertinent to our discussion. The reps of the company we're describing are expected to generate relationships with their accounts. The strategy of using channel partners for *manage* and *fulfill* activities is supposed to create enough time for sales reps to penetrate their accounts, find opportunities, and then turn them over to channel partners. In other words, the sales reps' primary job is to generate opportunities and gain what they call "customer mind-share" for their products, a strategy believed to offer reps more time to find additional opportunities.

This company's strategy provides an effective division of work for its salesforce and channel partners, both of which should benefit from the synergies created by all players when properly implemented. *But the strategy stops working when the supplier's reps approach all deals as if they are bids.* Bidding delays a trusted relationship because it positions the supplier on the bottom of the Value Staircase where price, not value, is most important.

Companies that pursue channels of distribution to sell their products should take notice and not emulate this kind of behavior. Neither party can focus on relationships because the supplier drags everyone into the fray of bidding and discounting. This leaves the door wide open to consultants, systems integrators, and other suppliers that are quick to jump on the inside track of becoming Trusted Advisors for these customers.

BIDDING IN ORBIT

We have advised against bidding whenever possible. Purchasing managers are supposed to buy things at the lowest price possible, and bidding offers them the perfect vehicle in which to discharge their duties. Next time you're in a purchasing department—perhaps start with your own—check if there are any signs on the wall that read "Trusted Relationships Start Here!" Also, next time you are in your boardroom, check to see if your CEO is displaying a sign that reads "We always strive to get the lowest price!" Get the point? Let's get on with our orbit story.

Do you remember John Glenn's heroic ride around the earth? The flight—the first of its kind—ran smoothly, but only one main concern on the ground cast a slight shadow over the event. Glenn's aircraft was covered with ceramic tiles that were installed to deflect the tremendous heat that would build on the craft's surface when it reentered the earth's atmosphere.

Concerns about the stability of those tiles were validated when the rocket began its reentry. The tiles began popping off as they overheated! And the craft completed its descent by landing in the ocean, where water was boiling around the capsule when the rescue boat arrived. Commander Glenn was taken swiftly to the recovery ship for tests and observation; he was healthy and safe.

When reporters were finally able to interview Glenn, one asked him to recall what was going through his mind as he reentered the atmosphere with the tiles popping off the craft. The reporter was obviously probing to see if the commander was thinking about the high points of his ride or of the inherent danger in his mission. But Glenn surprised them by saying, "What I was thinking on the way down—as the tiles were popping—was that the craft I was riding in was built by the lowest bidder!"

INTRODUCE YOURSELF

Rainmakers contribute their industry experience and business acumen to their clients' project team efforts, and so can you! Think about what you know how to do—where you have been—what you know—all that you have accomplished. Executives may perceive your knowledge and experience to be of extremely high value. That's why you need to find a way to introduce yourself to them. Executives like to kick around ideas when defining and documenting their issues, which is difficult when they're standing too close to those issues on a daily basis. Most executives wouldn't venture to entrust this diagnostic work to your sales reps, so take advantage of any opportunity to introduce your company's competencies in a nonsales surrounding. Remember, your products are merely tools to implement executives' solutions—they're almost an afterthought.

The profit margins rainmakers realize by prescribing your products are higher than any profit you will ever realize from selling them. And whatever profit you are getting can probably be increased if you move your involvement a step or two up the Value Staircase by finding ways to support the activities of a process team.

SUMMARY

Rainmakers realize higher margins for recommending your products than you will ever realize from innovating, designing, developing, marketing, and supporting them. They get these higher profit margins because they work as innovators. They *sell* everything, including your commodity products, whereas your salespeople *bid* them because they think the value has escaped as the products have aged. *Although the ultimate solution for a customer may be old news to the marketplace, it's brand-new and highly valued by a customer who uses it for the first time.*

While you are forced to tolerate the downward spiral of pricing and profit that naturally occurs over time, rainmakers operate on a higher plane. They do this by continually forcing themselves to push their customer pursuits to the left side of the Marketing Life Cycle. That kind of pursuit is equivalent to working at the top of the Value Staircase.

We hope you will begin to inspect the proposals that your sales teams are delivering to your customers. Look carefully at the pricing you are routinely offering, especially for your older commodities. Learn what logic is used to determine pricing. Assure yourself that deep discounts are offered only in extremely competitive situations and that your price will be the only determining factor in getting the business.

Most important of all, interview an executive in the company that's receiving your bids. Follow a rainmaker's lead and find out what your company could do to change that customer's perception of your product from *commodity* to *innovation* and your involvement from *bid* to *sell.*

CRM—BLESSING
OR CURSE?

Rainmakers often produce great data, but great data will never produce rainmakers. It's all about putting the horse before the cart! Implementation and management of CRM systems often becomes a main driver of corporate activity. The reality: CRM systems are only tools that measure and report results.

We can't close our book without commenting on CRM, or customer relationship management, systems. Everyone is excited about productivity tools for the new economy. Many Internet-based tools have created the potential for greater productivity in practically every industry and for practically every business function. Despite their obvious value, these tools can also cause people and businesses to run amok if they are not used appropriately. One potential area for this is CRM.

CRM systems are created and marketed by some of the technology industry's hottest companies, such as Oracle, PeopleSoft, and Siebel Systems. CRM systems feature computer applications that allow companies to register sales opportunities and then track those opportunities all the way through the sales cycle to whatever end point they reach. Sales reps are responsible for initially entering and constantly updating data regarding each prospective sales situation, a clerical task that can become onerous.

The functionality of the Internet makes it possible for all of your sales reps' customer and prospect data to be entered online, making it easy to import these sales data into your e-business application suite. Such suites are complex collections of applications that include financial, manufacturing, logistics, and other systems; and the Internet moves the data around at the speed of light. This capability should be a tremendous benefit to companies like yours that use these systems. So what could be the problem here?

The problem with CRM is the general perception of its purpose, not its content or capabilities. Many of the companies that have searched for years to find a process to help them build customer relationships seem to believe that making an investment in CRM solves that issue—that accumulating and analyzing sales data at the speed of light is tantamount to managing relationships. We believe that relationships must be built first, before CRM or any other Internet application systems can add value to them. Can you imagine how a computer tool could build or manage a relationship?

One big problem that we have seen with CRM systems is that they can turn unsuspecting executives, especially those in sales and marketing, into data analysts. Instead of spending time in their customers' offices, many executives now spend excessive amounts of time mulling over data that have been entered into their CRM systems by the same sales reps that haven't built executive relationships prior to the installation of the systems.

Many companies assume that a multi-million-dollar investment in CRM software makes sales reps more effective. Ask your reps if they are more effective at penetrating their accounts because of your CRM system. More to the point, ask your sales executives and managers how much time they spend in front of their computer screens, and then compare their answers to time they spend in front of your customers.

Sales reps we have interviewed display a universal dislike for CRM systems because the systems don't increase their face time with customers. They feel that these systems put them squarely in the middle of computer systems' implementation projects. They say that they have to spend too much time checking and entering data, and that time must be deducted from time they could be spending with customers. In a nutshell, they feel that these CRM systems don't benefit them directly. So we must ask: Whom do they benefit?

Let's examine how a complete implementation of CRM in a suite of e-business software can increase productivity if handled correctly. A simplified view of a business process enabled by these software applications might work as follows:

A sales rep finds a sales opportunity and promptly logs it into the CRM system. An estimated date to close the deal is entered along with the rep's estimated odds that it will close. All such opportunities, entered by all reps, are rolled up into a gross forecast. At the gross level, if a total of $10 million of opportunities is forecast at an average of 60 percent odds, then the opportunity backlog is assumed to be worth $6 million. Specific product model information and requested dates for customer delivery are then rolled up and exported into the company's financial models and manufacturing systems. Raw materials are forecast and ordered at a level dependent on the company's tolerance for inventory risk. Historical data are available in the system to help make those decisions.

When sales are made, customers can place their orders online. Next, the orders are compared to the sales forecast database. Once matched, the orders are electronically exported to the manufacturing and logistics systems, where the products are manufactured, packaged, and shipped. The manufacturing facility is often a third-party contracted function, so the invoicing and billing systems send the proper documentation as a follow-up, and then all databases are updated for the transaction. Any subsequent technical support is provided online as well, and the great majority of support questions are handled by databases with no human intervention.

It's not unusual these days to hear companies bragging about their new economy orientation. Many claim to have saved millions of dollars through the use of electronic systems. Their products are built to order and shipped to their customers, and *no employee in their company ever touches the customer, the order, or the completed product.* That's real productivity for sure, but what might a company lose through these practices? What might a company lose when it replaces "human touch" with "technology touch?" It's one thing for a company to provide customers with a means to access their order backlog, service requests, or accounts receivable balance. But is it wise to replace human touch when it is such an important building block in customer relationships?

Can you build a relationship with someone you never "touch?" Michael Dell, CEO of Dell Computer, attributes much of his company's success to the fact that they have never lost touch with their end users. Dell is extremely advanced in its use of technology in every aspect of its business, but it has always maintained its customer touch by entrusting sales goals to its own sales reps. Dell has never put technology between his company and his customers.

Don Imus, the nationally syndicated radio host, in November 2002 asked IBM's recently retired Lou Gerstner what he would do differently at IBM if he could go back and do it all again. Gerstner thought a moment and then replied, "I'd sell PCs direct—with our own sales reps—instead of distributing them into the channel." Gerstner stated clearly that IBM could have benefited greatly had it maintained human touch with its PC customers.

Computer databases grow exponentially as a company's transactions increase, and this growth in the quantity of data makes it possible to analyze the data in a number of mind-boggling ways. Used properly, all of these historical data help managers improve their command of their business, both future and past. It's also possible for managers to become so absorbed in data and data analysis that they find themselves delegating important duties and functions to employees who have neither the skills nor experience to accomplish them. This is often the case with CRM.

Our up-front assessment of CRM is that sales reps usually hate it, and executives and managers become trapped by their expectations of it. CRM is very expensive to implement and is usually one of any company's largest technology investments. Top-level managers are used to being measured on their ability to maximize the returns they get on large investments, but this becomes problematic with CRM because the effectiveness of the investment is difficult to measure.

Executives find that CRM applications produce more data about their forecasts and other sales activities than they have ever seen before, so someone has to take the time to analyze and understand all of those data. Because they are the ones who buy these systems, executives often wind up spending a disproportionate share of their time looking at the data. By the way, we have never met any sales executives, sales managers, or sales reps who have begged to have CRM implemented.

We believe that sales reps are at odds with top-level business managers about CRM because of several basic issues. First, CRM requires sales reps to enter as much data as possible about every potential sales situation in their territories. In many salesforces, the *quantity* of data entered is treated with greater importance than the *quality* of the data. Sales reps are paid for results, and data entry doesn't put bread on the table.

Second, managers generate reports and forecasts based on the data the reps enter, and these reports become the primary communication vehicles for customer reviews and dialogue. Reps know that most account management is an art, not a science; and CRM doesn't allow subjective, qualitative dialogue.

Third, CRM forecasts and reports are typically made available to all managers in all areas of a company. Thanks to the way these Internet applications are integrated, all data become ubiquitous in all areas of a business. That tends to create many sales "experts" within a company, and many of these new experts have never met a customer. Yet they analyze, integrate, and report customer data. Worse, they may make decisions on the data alone.

Sales reps and their managers naturally worry when they see their management teams analyzing the data that they have provided. Many nuances that influence the accuracy and legitimacy of the conclusions that are reached in their reports are not comprehended in management's analysis. Most companies don't attempt to distinguish bids from higher-value opportunities in their analyses because data input screens don't comprehend the difference. For this reason, bids show the highest close rate because the opportunities are more concrete; and this in turn encourages more bidding.

Fourth, all sales reps will tell you that the quality of their opportunities doesn't increase simply because they enter data about them over the Internet. It bothers them to see the amount of time that their managers spend analyzing the data, and they often live in fear that the data they supply will be used as a club if they don't accomplish the tasks that the system says they should and accomplish them within the prescribed time frame.

GREAT DATA—BAD APPLICATION

CRM reminds me of an incident involving a young sales rep we met after a seminar a few years ago. He wanted to show us the incredible amount of data that he had accumulated about one of his customers. His database included the results of a lot of research about the customer's business, competitors, and industry segment. He had organized the data into several segments and was preparing a presentation for the customer.

When I asked this young rep what he was going to do with all of those data, he replied, "I'm going to present them to my customer's management team at a briefing next week." He was shocked when I suggested that he was making a mistake, that he was using his data incorrectly. He naturally wanted to know what was wrong with his approach, so I reminded him: "They already know all of that stuff! It's their business. It's only news to you!"

This guy was baffled how to use all of the data that CRM required him to accumulate. If he couldn't use the data on sales calls, then what use could the data be to him? That, in a nutshell, is the primary reason that sales reps dislike CRM systems. They feel they enter data for everyone's benefit but their own. It's hard to be supportive of an activity from which you gain no personal benefit.

Sales and marketing executives we have served through the years are often resentful that CRM systems keep them chained to their computer monitors. The ubiquity of sales forecast data forces them to stay in their office because they have to answer the phone when the boss calls and asks for an update, and bosses who are armed with lots of data call their sales managers with great frequency. When everyone has data, more questions are apt to be asked.

PLAY THE GAME

To oversimplify this situation, let's say that analyses of recent historical sales data show that 40 percent of opportunities in the pipeline will close within any 30-day period. That means the salesforce can be counted on to close $400,000 for every $1 million that is forecast. We have seen cases where top management does its financial planning based on ratios that are supplied by financial analysts who pour over sales history, calculate ratios, and *never show them to the salesforce!* Assuming that the company wants to achieve a lot of growth, sales reps will then have to increase the number of dollars they forecast into the pipeline, hoping the current 40 percent close ratio applies to the new, higher volumes being forecast.

As with any other business concept, quality can be diminished when volume grows. So as the company grows, analyses will most likely show that the rate of closure for pipeline dollars erodes from 40 percent to a lesser number, perhaps 30 percent. At this point the sales department realizes it is closing a lower percentage of a number that is increasing. So the dilemma of what to do is solved by simply entering more data; and soon the quantity of data has exploded, but the quality of the inputs has eroded.

Sales and marketing executives tell us that their bosses often draw the wrong conclusions from their CRM reports. They worry because these reports are generated from data that are entered when their sales reps are under pressure to forecast enough to achieve their goals. But the sales managers don't know what to do about it. Many of them have told us they don't dare speak negatively about their CRM systems, because that would be seen as questioning the validity of the huge investment that had been made in the systems.

RAINMAKERS AND CRM

By stating our position on CRM data gathering and analysis, we don't mean to imply that rainmakers don't accumulate and store data about their clients. They do, in fact, accumulate large storehouses of data about their clients and the engagements they perform with them. See Appendix D for examples. Many rainmakers have organized practices around implementing CRM for their clients, and many of these rainmakers use CRM systems in their own practice. Their credentials, in fact, include CRM knowledge and experience.

The fundamental difference between rainmakers' use of CRM and their clients' use of these systems is clear. Rainmakers personally contribute client data to their databases along with everyone else on their teams. They are personally involved in engagements with their clients, so they can balance the data submitted by others with their own experiences and first-hand observations. In other words, rainmakers don't rely solely on electronic inputs from others to keep them informed about customer and sales issues. This is dramatically different from the way most businesses implement and use their CRM systems. As with so many of the customer-oriented processes we've referred to in this book, rain-makers lead by example—business leaders delegate.

How does it work in your company? If you are an executive, do you know where the customer and sales data you look at originate? Do you know who has seen the data before you; how the data have been diluted, manipulated, or scrubbed? Do you have personal access to the data input portion of your CRM system, and do you (or your assistant) add data every time you meet with a customer executive—even if only to shake hands and conduct a social discourse? Does it sometimes bother you when your gut rumbles after interactions with customers because your radar tells you that the prospects for doing business aren't quite as bull-ish as your data reviews suggested?

A CHALLENGE

We are issuing this challenge to all of our executive readers who rely on CRM reports as their sole source of information about their customers:

Suspend your reliance on CRM data until you have personally entered customer data that you have gathered in a peer-level interview with one customer executive.

That's where the substantive data will be found. Your CRM data will be more accurate when you personally augment it with data that are based on your personal encounters with customers. Executives, hear this! Your personal involvement with customers will make your CRM data more actionable, and your conversations with your sales managers will become more productive because you will have a common point of reference. If you are familiar with a customer, your salespeople will spend less time trying to pull the wool over your eyes. That's part of the advantage rainmakers have over you and your sales staff today. But you can change all that by becoming more of a rainmaker yourself.

PEEL THE ONION AND SEE THE PROBLEM

"Peeling the onion" graphically exposes the problem with "technology touching." (See Figure 14.1.) The supplier's first point of contact with customers, who are appropriately seated in the center of the universe, is a technology interface of some kind, perhaps an order-entry screen. Sales reps are the next level of touch, where they gather data and input it into the CRM system. Customers are also touched by other pieces of the supplier's electronic systems as well as the product support function.

The arrangement just described leads management to view accounts through the lens of its technology systems, which repositions management to analyze the growing amounts of data entered by reps and customers. At the outside of the diagram, you'll find the top executives, who have to be the final backstop for all of the data in this situation.

The illustration in Figure 14.2 replaces the technology interface with a rainmaker as the first point of engagement. Many business leaders will

FIGURE 14.1 *Technology Touch*

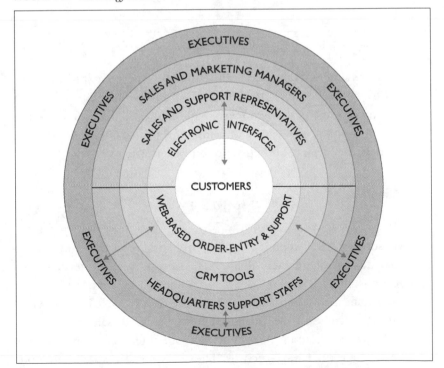

FIGURE 14.2 *Human Touch*

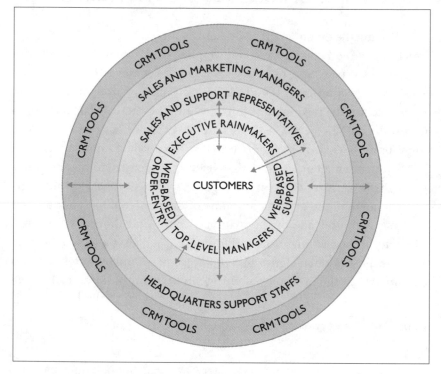

cringe at this suggestion because of the time they perceive it will take, although executive briefings and other programs we highlighted earlier could mitigate some of their concern. Note that CRM is now at the outer edge of the model, so instead of being the primary business drivers, technology tools are properly positioned as reporting tools.

SUMMARY

We support CRM when it's implemented as a reporting and analysis tool. Slicing and dicing data will always be necessary, and Internet-based applications, like CRM, allow people in all areas of a company to share common data, thus eliminating redundancies. Giving it its due, CRM does mitigate some of the problems newly assigned salespeople have when they need accurate information about their new territories but can't find the former reps' records. These CRM systems also help companies protect their customer data by institutionalizing them, securing the data into databases so they don't "walk out" of the company when reps leave. And historical close rates for sales forecasts, easily computed from CRM files, can provide important information that helps other areas of a business forecast their activities with greater accuracy.

Our concern with CRM, therefore, is not about functionality. On the basis of the systems we have observed, they do exactly what they are supposed to do from a technical standpoint. *The problem: CRM systems can get in the way of the very relationships they are supposed to help.* Collecting data about customers doesn't draw you closer to them. CRM doesn't manage relationships, so calling it customer *relationship* management may be an oxymoron. Because CRM actually manages data about customers, regardless of whether a relationship exists, "CDM," or *customer data management,* is probably a more accurate description of what these systems deliver. The idea that a computer system can manage a relationship is incorrect by any measure we can imagine.

We hope that our clients find ways to capitalize on the huge investments they have made in CRM, and we hope that CRM suppliers will take the lead in positioning these products more carefully so that their customers find as many benefits for sales reps as for executive sponsors.

Executives and other top-level managers may find that the CRM trap makes it more difficult to devote the necessary time to being rainmakers. Sales managers and reps, playing the data analysis game, can also burn precious time working and managing the increasing volumes of data that they create, all of which detracts from the amount of "face time" they can spend with their customers. Sales reps around the globe could make this book an instant best-seller if their executives would read it first and then allow the reps to suggest changes to their CRM systems without fear of penalty.

15

FINAL THOUGHTS

We hope that you are figuring out how to begin implementing a Pyramid. It's a normal reaction if you're not quite sure where to start. Overcoming the confusion is far more important than wondering *if* you should do it.

Sometimes we get so excited about helping you develop new relationships that we forget to distinguish between making new customer contacts and creating new relationships with the loyal customers that you already have. These ideas are not mutually exclusive. In fact, the best way to start your Pyramid is by focusing first on the good customers you already have. Remember the old song lyrics?

Make new friends, but keep the old. The new are silver and the old are gold.

The greater the loyalty a company engenders among its current customers, the greater the profits it reaps. In his books *The Loyalty Effect* and *Loyalty Rules!* (Harvard Business School Press, 2001), Frederick Reichheld documents the outstanding results generated by leaders who built a measurable advantage in customer loyalty. By analyzing the economic forces that link loyalty to profits, he explains the enormous growth and cost advantages inherent in building loyalty. Reichheld demonstrates why, in industry after industry, the high cost of acquiring customers renders many customer relationships unprofitable during their early years. Only in later years, when the cost of serving loyal customers falls and revenue increases, do relationships generate big returns.

> *The bottom line: An increase of 5 percent in customer retention has been shown to increase profits by 25 percent to 95 percent.*

Building on the work of more than a decade, Reichheld's most recent research points to certain facts that many executives may not want to hear. A study of "Loyalty Leaders"—companies with the most impressive loyalty credentials—indicates that the challenge of engendering loyalty cannot be delegated to a task force or middle-level management. It cannot be addressed by a new CRM system, having a better customer database, measurement systems, or reward programs.

Outstanding marks for customer loyalty are earned when executives are willing to demonstrate their personal commitment to customers on a daily basis. The companies that Reichheld studied didn't skimp on talent, technology, or strategy, but it was clearly the interaction with customers at the executive level that drove the loyalty factor.

WARY EXECUTIVES

Although executives may seem comfortable participating in an interview with a consulting partner, most are wary of spending the same amount of time with salespeople. Many executives started their career in sales, which means they understand what's happening when a sales rep leads them into a manipulative process. Executives may not resent those actions, but they don't see them as enhancing trust either! We hope you now have an appreciation for the degree of consistency that exists in rainmakers' methods and processes. Executives know what to expect from a partner, senior manager, or manager from a consulting firm; salespeople are usually not so predictable.

One reason executives avoid sales calls is that they are not responsible for selecting products for their company; instead, they ponder strategic issues. Product discussions are difficult to force onto an executive's calendar for that reason, and sales reps who claim to have solutions don't make the situation better. In fact, having a canned solution to a problem that has stymied an executive for weeks or months can make the executive feel a little foolish. After all, if it's so simple that a canned solution can be packaged, why is an executive spending so much time on it?

THE SCOOP ON SALES REPS

We love sales reps. We revere them! And we know they provide the most value when they work in the *manage* phase of the Marketing Cycle, addressing the customer demand that is building among users and operational managers in the majority (see Figure 5.2). It is not demeaning to sales reps to ask them to cover the middle and lower levels of the Value Staircase. Fact is, that's where the vast majority of them spend all of their time anyway. *The greatest lesson of the Pyramid: Cover your customers' entire organization.*

We contend sales reps are more productive when they have "artillery support" from top managers—when their executives cover their customers' top steps on the Value Staircase. A Pyramid slots executives, managers, and individual contributors in their most effective zones when matching them up to customer opportunities.

MAKE A CONSCIOUS CHOICE

We believe that you should make a conscious choice to send the appropriate representative every time you decide to contact one of your valued customers. You can put your sales reps into the breech every time and expect them to create a dialogue at all of the critical levels within the customers' organization. But as you know, we believe your better choice is to view each potential customer contact as a rainmaker would. Determine who in your organization is most likely to share common experiences and issues with the customer manager in question.

Instituting a peer-level matchup process doesn't assume that sales reps should be left entirely out of the loop. In fact, the reps can be perceived as extremely trustworthy when they are operating in the proper context—that is, they should keep their focus on the lower-middle and bottom of the Value Staircase—driving positive customer satisfaction results with the operational, tactical managers that use your products.

Earlier we suggested that sales reps provide their best return when they are selling mature products to majority customers in the manage phase of the marketing life cycle. Reps tend to work best with end users of your products, and they also work well with purchasing managers, with whom they can focus on customers' procurement and support issues. Remember, your company needs to build trusted relationships at the user and purchasing department levels, too. Taking reps out of their normal routines and pushing them into executive offices jeopardizes these important relationships.

Most user department managers and purchasing managers are found on the lower levels of the Value Staircase. Go back to Figure 5.1 to see how rainmakers match up these people. Your sales reps, sales managers, and field support personnel are analogous to consultants' staff and senior staff people.

THE PEACH BOWL

The true story on page 209 illustrates the importance of peer-level relationships, and it demonstrates how opportunities for customer relationships often originate outside the four walls of a company. Sometimes the best opportunities present themselves when you least expect them. Many opportunities occur at social and community functions where peers are involved with each other for reasons other than business. It's rare when a sales rep is present in one of these situations.

Think about the social and community involvement opportunities surrounding your management team members on a regular basis, and try to assess how your relationship-building effectiveness could change positively if your top managers acted or reacted like rainmakers. This real example occurred at a football game!

His team was very large and included senior-level account executives, sales reps, systems engineers, and administrative personnel. They managed many millions of dollars of IBM's assets in their account, but they had never met the chairman. After the holidays, I ventured back into IBM's Atlanta offices and attempted to report what I thought was good

A T r u e S t o r y

My wife and I settled in Atlanta, Georgia, in the early 1990s. Jerry Bartels, a great friend of ours who was president of the Atlanta Chamber of Commerce, invited us to attend the annual Peach Bowl college football game with his wife and "a few business friends." Jerry told us that he had the good fortune to get us invited to watch the game in a luxury skybox that was owned by one of Atlanta's best-known, most prestigious companies.

We arrived, were greeted at the door by the president of the company and his wife, and then I proceeded to pour myself a drink at the self-service bar. As I stood there trying to locate the football field through the crowded room, a gentleman approached me and shook my hand; I quickly realized he was the CEO of our host company. He asked me what line of work I was engaged in, and I told him that I was a consultant. "Oh yeah, you must be out of work," was his reply. I assured him that I had real clients, and he asked me who was my biggest client. When I responded that IBM was taking most of my time, he looked surprised for a moment. Then he replied with a very few words that are etched in my memory:

> *Really! You work with IBM? Listen, you've probably read in the newspapers that we may have to lay off some employees for the first time in our history. As with IBM, we have always provided careers for life. The implications of doing this are huge for our whole industry. I think that IBM has a lead on us in resolving their people issues, and I've been curious about how they have approached the issue. Do you think anyone from IBM would talk with us about what it's done?*

That was all there was to it. The whole conversation took about as long as it took you to read about it. I didn't see him again during the evening. In fact, I never saw him again. But there's more to the story.

About two weeks before the Peach Bowl, I had conducted a consultative selling seminar for some IBM account teams in Atlanta. About midway through the three-day session, an account executive seated at a front table raised his hand, stood up, and said, "This is all well and good for companies whose executives get involved with their customers. It may work for some of these people, but our account is so huge that I can assure you no one at the top has any interest in anything we have to say!" Could you see it coming? I asked him what account he and his team were responsible for, and he replied with the name of our Peach Bowl host!

news. After all, the CEO of one of the team's largest accounts had asked a question that was right in the team's sweet spot. What could be better than that?

After my brief report, the first question the account exec asked me was, "Why are you doing this? What's in it for you?" I told him that we had long ago finished being "a pair of hands" to his company. We had invested time being "therapists," and many managers in IBM treated us as "collaborators." This was an opportunity to collaborate; that was what was in it for us.

I reminded him about the Pyramid discussion in the seminar and suggested this was one of those rare chances to establish a level of contact higher up on the Value Staircase with his account. I suggested that he might consider inviting one of IBM's top human resources managers to join him in a meeting with the CEO. He told me that they didn't use human resources people on customer sales calls. In fact, because this involved the CEO, he wondered if he had to have IBM's chairman make the call. But he was concerned that his chairman was too busy to make "human resources calls." The account exec didn't want to raise a major issue up through his chain of command.

Question: What would a rainmaker from a firm like PricewaterhouseCoopers (PWC) have done if he or she had attended the same football party and heard the CEO's question? We believe that a PWC rainmaker attending the party would have sought out the CEO for an informal interview at the same bar where I was standing. Partners run into opportunities like this one all the time; it's a cultural thing with them.

I can't help believing that the outcome would've been very different if IBM CEO Lou Gerstner had attended that football party. Had that been the case, I have total confidence he would have called one of his top human resources staff members, probably that weekend at home, and asked the person to join him for a meeting in Atlanta. Why? Because Gerstner would want to help the other executive, and he'd probably learn something as well. Gerstner's background includes a stint at McKinsey & Company, where he was a rainmaker. "Once a rainmaker, always a rainmaker."

I have no way of knowing if the IBM account team would have capitalized on the opportunity if one of its top local sales directors had been there. But I do know that many opportunities like this present themselves on a regular basis to executives, including yours, when they become involved with their local ballets, symphonies, chambers of commerce, and other business organizations.

We have seen many a traditional business like yours become hamstrung with policies, practices, and red tape that prevent executive-to-executive dialogues. That's a cultural thing as well, and it was definitely the case at IBM in the early 1990s. IBM began to change all of that when Gerstner forced the company to develop and execute a strategy to produce more of its results through services rather than through selling hardware. This services strategy, in turn, rewarded rainmaker behavior, and it moved the company a long way toward adopting a peer-level matchup mentality that was critical in turning the company around. As we mentioned earlier, much of Gerstner's legacy at IBM is about rainmaking and reestablishing trust with customers.

Can you recall any examples like our Peach Bowl story where you and your executives might have fallen into similar opportunities? A corporate executive that we spent a lot of time with related his feelings about peer-level contacts as follows:

I frequently feel the need for help. I want to be able to kick around issues with someone I can trust, someone who has faced the same kinds of issues. I don't care if they have succeeded in resolving the issues. The fact that they've just faced them is enough.

I asked him why he preferred not to talk to his own staff members about these things, and he replied:

They haven't had to deal with the kinds of issues I deal with. They have no experience. They rely on me to handle them. They only tell me what I want to hear anyway, so their input is not worth much.

I didn't ask him if he would consider kicking his issues around with a supplier's sales reps. That may sound flippant, but isn't that the assumption you make when you tell your sales reps to "call at the top"?

HOW FAR WILL YOU GO?

In closing, we'd like to challenge you to think about making the Pyramid work in your business. We know that you can foster more Trust in your key customer relationships by doing this. Start slowly. Think about the value of finding a common ground with just one customer executive who works at your level, and conduct yourself in a way that enables the two of you to develop a genuine respect for each other. We contend that trust will be easier to establish with presidents when they are enabled to have a dialogue with your president, assuming the intended dialogue is of a strategic nature. That common ground and respect you establish will encourage empathy to develop in both directions, unlike the results that are usually achieved with the manipulative FFF behavior we referred to earlier.

When you position yourself to develop this kind of empathy with a peer-level customer executive, you will find yourself naturally engaging in the following kinds of actions—all of which will become the foundation for your *relationship advantage:*

- Communicating about up-to-date information on the industry, the market, or a specific business topic
- Working through a laundry list of common, difficult problems: make or buy; acquire or divest; revise a strategy; organizational alignment; financial policy; compensation; morale; operational efficiency
- Engaging in a diagnostic dialogue that examines the business and personal issues surrounding key decisions and results
- Helping think through the objectives and needed actions when addressing a critical business problem and the challenges in achieving significant results
- Coaching about building consensus and commitment around problem definition, corrective action, and a process to effect change
- Transferring knowledge about dealing with immediate issues and methods that can address future challenges

GETTING STARTED

Ask yourself, Which of my current customers would let me try a Pyramid approach? Where could you institute peer-level matchups with other executives that are strategically important to you and, at the same time, incur the least amount of risk? Once you have selected a customer for this trial, reread our chapters "The Best-Kept Secret" and "Questions" to get yourself primed and ready to go. Even though we recommend researching the customer you select, you also have an acceptable fallback position in questioning companies that have bought a lot of products from you in the past.

The fallback works like this: You will find that your salespeople are able to tell you *what* they have sold to each one of their customers month by month for the past decade. Most sales analysis systems are that good; but few reps will be able to tell you *why* your customers bought your products. They won't know which of the customers' departments justified the procurements; what the customers' expected return on investment (ROI) was on the purchase; which executive sponsored the purchase; and, most important, how the sponsoring executive feels about the investment after the purchase.

These are the kinds of questions you can probe with a customer's executive team. The only way to obtain answers is to ask, and we hope you can see the wisdom of asking executives, not a manager in the purchasing department or an operations manager who uses the product or a financial analyst who reports to the controller's office.

Approaching a large customer on your first rainmaker assignment might prove difficult. In a perfect world your CEO would contact a large customer's president and conduct a diagnostic interview, but that's not likely to happen at first. We therefore suggest that you or another of your top-level managers approach a peer-level customer manager in a smaller account with whom you have some familiarity. Call and schedule an appointment; you'll likely have to divulge the subject of the appointment, so make it easy on yourself and say that you'd like to get an "executive perspective" on the customer satisfaction data the company provided you—a perspective that can't be given by the people who filled out the survey. Another plausible reason for seeking an appointment is to compare notes on ways to resolve a certain business issue that you have in common with that customer. Avoid saying you came by simply to say "Hello," because few executives have time for courtesy calls these days.

We hope we made the case with you for researching your customers before you make an approach. In addition to researching facts about the company you select, we're suggesting that you should invest whatever time is necessary to understand *how* each of your major sales took place and *why* they occurred. Many pages of data about major procurements probably exist in your computer databases, so start your research there. Remember, just because a company buys your products doesn't mean that you have developed mutual understanding and respect with that company as well; in fact, many tried and true customers are unfortunately taken for granted.

You'll likely discover through your research and questioning that your products were procured to fulfill part of a solution after someone else's rainmaker conducted a business process reengineering project. Planning teams have already worked through a multitude of problems and issues together and concluded they needed your products. It's hoped you'll find that the reengineering work is ongoing, giving you an opportunity to find a way to participate. You need to be included only once to discover how critical this kind of activity is to your future success.

We hate to beat a dead horse, but please *do not delegate this assignment to your salesforce.* Customer executives are in the habit of turning away from appointments with your sales reps, but they won't know quite what to do with your request for an appointment, so they'll probably honor it. Don't be discouraged if they decline your idea. Move on to another executive and so on until you succeed. We know from experience that getting an appointment is not a problem. The problem is getting the second appointment—getting invited back again!

Remember that you'll have to reset the mood of the meeting as soon as you enter the other executive's office. Will you try to be interest*ing*, or will you choose to be interest*ed*? Does the prospect of doing this create butterflies in your stomach? Choosing the interest*ed* option will alleviate many of those butterflies because the other executive will be the performer if you handle your assignment correctly. Again, the information we provided in the chapters "The Best-Kept Secret," "Questions," "Go East," and "Diagnose and Prescribe" will help you prepare for and execute this interview.

CONCLUSION

The Relationship Advantage is a road map for traditional business executives and managers who realize they can achieve competitive advantage by becoming *Trusted Advisors* to their customers. The journey starts with the realization that having customers doesn't mean the same thing as having relationships, especially the kinds of relationships that will insulate a business when times get tough or when a competitor produces a better mousetrap.

We urge traditional companies like yours to implement the attributes and processes we outlined in this book to improve your business results. You'll improve your chances of building trusted relationships in the course of conducting your daily business. Being practitioners of the Wheel of Fortune ourselves, we suggest the following course of action to all of our executive readers who want to build Trusted Relationships with their customers:

- Conduct research about your customers, starting with your current best customers. We leave the definition of *best* to your judgment: It could refer to customers that have stuck with you for the longest periods of time; customers that have bought the most; customers whose purchases have provided the highest profit margins; or customers that are not profitable but have strategic importance. The point is to research them; know them; and understand their market, their competition, and their industry.

- Think about the research information you obtain. Analyze it the way you believe your customers analyze it. Develop an understanding of their greatest unresolved issues.

- Interview one, two, or three customer executives. Ask them process questions about the information you obtain. Suspend your sales reps' routine sales calls on these trial accounts until you have executed an interview. Invite your sales reps and others who are familiar with the trial accounts to participate in the data gathering; that's how your mentoring program can start.

- Try to qualify some of the current business opportunities that have been brought to the table by your salespeople. Before releasing proposals, check the base propositions against the Opportunity Assessment Matrix we outlined in Chapter 6 (Figure 6.2). Understand where your current hunger for deals is leading you. See if you're committing your company to lowering its future expectations by planting too many easy roots. This is mentoring that can take place early in the game.

- Start an informal audit of your CRM system to understand how it may be pushing your management team away from strategic activities in order to make tactical numbers. Ask your reps to give you an honest assessment of the system's worth. Find out where the sales data are going and how they're being used as well as how much time your executive team is spending trying to make sense of the data.

We are convinced that business relationships are built on mutual respect and trust; and rainmakers are good role models for such building. Every one of you possesses the interpersonal skills needed to create relationships, because we know that each one of you has formed relationships in your personal lives.

Finally, think once again about the meaningful relationships you currently enjoy apart from your career. How have you succeeded in presenting your ideas and thoughts—and avoided asking trite, insincere questions—in those personal relationships? Most people we have quizzed characterize their personal relationships as "warm," "fuzzy," "finding mutual interests," "sharing mutual problems," and "enjoying our time together." We're not suggesting that all of your business relationships should run that deep, but we are suggesting that business relationships do rely on mutual interests and mutual respect. Business colleagues can enjoy their time together if the time is structured correctly.

What are you going to do to improve your relationships with your customers? How can you change your approach so that the most important customers become "clients"? What are your two or three best reasons for making that happen? What ammunition have we given you to help you do it?

Let us know what more we can do to help you undertake this important, strategic journey. We are *interested!*

COMPETENCY PROFILES FOR CONSULTANTS

COMPETENCY PROFILES FOR STAFF/SENIOR STAFF AND MANAGER/SENIOR MANAGER

I. CORE COMPETENCIES

Evaluation Category

- *Familiarity with:* sales & marketing, finance, operations; other disciplines; other consulting services; overall business operations of client.

- *Analytical skills:* problem identification on timely basis, ability to evaluate alternatives and to develop solutions.

- *Communications:* writing grammar, structure; ability and ease in giving and receiving oral instructions; clarity and conciseness; listening, attentiveness, responsiveness.

- *Business consciousness:* ability to recognize new opportunities; willingness and skill in contributing to developing work.

Is the Staff/Senior Consultant Capable of . . .

- Establishing a primary level of experience and taking a lead role in at least one consulting discipline, service, or industry?

- Understanding the overall functions of key business activities?

- Communicating effectively in oral, written, and visual presentations as part of an overall project team?

- Preparing major sections or complete volumes of project work products and reports?

- Recognizing opportunities and assisting in securing additional work, either as follow-up to existing engagements or as new work?

- Participating in planning and preparing proposals and work plans?

Is the Manager/Senior Manager Capable of . . .

- Demonstrating outstanding technical knowledge in one or more consulting disciplines, services, or industries?

- Demonstrating a good working knowledge of other consulting disciplines and identifying areas requiring additional expertise?

- Staying current on latest developments in his or her area of specialization?

- Coordinating with consulting team on a regular basis regarding specific engagement activities?

- Maintaining ongoing communication and professional relationships with key client personnel?

- Making presentations to large client and industry groups?

- Preparing executive-level as well as detailed client reports?

- Initiating, planning, and carrying out well-conceived consulting practice development activities?

- Developing add-on engagements and realizing opportunities for carrying out multiple projects in different problem areas for the same client?

2. WORKING CHARACTERISTICS

Evaluation Category

- *Production of high-quality results:* exercise judgment as to which decisions require further approval or concurrence; dependability, response to pressure; productivity, capacity for work.

Is the Staff/Senior Consultant Capable of ...

- Deciding on content and organization of engagement work products and documentation?

- Making key engagement decisions in the absence of the Director, surfacing critical issues for review based on priorities, and developing alternative suggestions for resolution?

Is the Manager/Senior Manager Capable of ...

- Effectively managing multiple consultants on various types of concurrent engagements?

- Initiating and assisting in the development of consulting products and standardized work products?

- Effectively reviewing and approving work products and maintaining the proper level of quality control?

3. ENGAGEMENT ADMINISTRATION

Evaluation Category

- *Organization aspects:* planning; executing; following instructions; keeping team informed; completing assignment on timely basis. Appropriate coordination with client, partner, and engagement team.

- *Financial aspects:* budgeting and controlling time; keeping team informed.

Is the Staff/Senior Consultant Capable of ...

- Planning important segments of large engagements or entire smaller projects and instructing the team and monitoring and reviewing work of others?

- Monitoring time spent on various assigned tasks and making judgments and informing the director as the impact of changes in scope and timing on the project budget?

- Working on a series of multiple engagements on a concurrent basis without jeopardizing the results of any one at the expense of another?

Is the Manager/Senior Manager Capable of . . .

- Deciding proposal and engagement strategies relating to all aspects and phases of work including establishing deliverables, work plans, staffing requirements, and fee estimates?

- Initiating and being fully responsible for planning and administering multiple consulting engagements of varying size and complexity?

- Billing and collecting fees in accordance with planned fee arrangements and conducting fee negotiations with key client personnel?

4. PEOPLE DEVELOPMENT

Evaluation Category

- *Leadership:* acceptance of responsibility; setting example for team.

- *Delegation:* establishing objectives; spreading work opportunities efficiently and fairly.

- *Training:* providing guidance on work delegated, reviewing and evaluating performance of team, preparing performance evaluations; timeliness of submission.

Is the Staff/Senior Consultant Capable of . . .

- Providing clear instructions to other team members and assigning meaningful project activities to others?

- Monitoring and comprehensively reviewing the work of other team members as engagements progress?

- Effectively delegating work and providing consulting leadership?

- Preparing meaningful consulting performance reports and discussing them effectively with team members?

Is the Manager/Senior Manager Capable of . . .

- Assigning project responsibilities to team members in a manner that provides them with challenge and growth, while maintaining project quality?

- Assisting team members in developing key technical, administrative and interpersonnel knowledge and skills?

- Providing clear instructions to consultants and monitoring progress of assigned tasks?

- Preparing meaningful consulting performance reports and effectively developing consultants through discussion, coaching, and career counseling?

- Monitoring and comprehensively reviewing the work of team members and providing timely feedback as engagements progress?

5. PERSONAL CHARACTERISTICS

Evaluation Categories

- Professional image and appearance

- Poise and maturity, self-confidence

- Independence

- Integrity

- Interpersonal skills: client, associates

- Self-motivation, initiative

- Attitude toward firm

Is the Staff/Senior Consultant Capable of . . .

- Developing the confidence of the client?

- Obtaining advanced professional certification and progressing toward leadership in appropriate organizations?

- Maintaining a high level of morale for all team members during all aspects of a project (e.g., team spirit, overtime, multiple commitments)?

Is the Manager/Senior Manager Capable of . . .

- Developing the confidence of top client officials?

- Representing the firm well in a variety of client and industry group situations?

- Maintaining a "can do" professional attitude throughout all types of situations and providing a role model for team members?

- Motivating team members to outstanding levels of performance and establishing the respect of his or her peers?

- Interacting with clients and associates in a clear, mature, and professional manner?

COMPETENCY PROFILE FOR PARTNER

Evaluation Category	*Qualifications*
CHARACTER AND INTEGRITY	• Professional stature in consulting • Motivated by own professionalism • Job satisfaction derived from client satisfaction
LEADERSHIP	• Viewed with a high degree of respect and confidence by consulting staff and clients • Demonstrated staff training and development results • Demonstrated practice and engagement results
INDEPENDENCE AND IMPARTIALITY OF MIND	• Team player • Willingness to express minority review • Success in building on previous experience
TECHNICAL KNOWLEDGE AND SKILL	• Team player • Willingness, general working knowledge in other disciplines • Quality of engagement work products • Demonstrated high level of productivity
ADMINISTRATIVE ABILITY AND BUSINESS JUDGMENT	• Project management skills on multidiscipline engagements • Demonstrated results to client • Engagement results measured in terms of skill and staff development, client satisfaction, and economic results

Evaluation Category	*Qualifications*
ABILITY TO PLAN CONSTRUCTIVELY FOR THE FUTURE	• Self-development record • Initiation of new practice aids • Initiation of new and innovative engagement approaches
ADAPTABILITY TO STRESS AND STRAIN	• Ability to see engagement in proper perspective and deal with issues of scope • Response to problem engagements
ABILITY TO ATTRACT NEW CLIENTS	• Practice development results • Continuing series of engagements for existing clients • High level of demand for self and staff
ARTICULATENESS	• Communication skills—oral and written • Listening skills
CAPACITY FOR FUTURE GROWTH	• Demonstrated rapid progress in learning grid • Ability to deal with unknown areas • Willingness to research • Self-development record
CREATIVITY	• Ability to develop innovative approaches • Results and value thereof of innovative approaches • Idea generation
INITIATIVE	• Self-development record • Willingness to undertake difficult, high-risk engagements • High degree of flexibility

CREATION CYCLE TACTICS

What do you want to know that wasn't in the RFP or inquiry?

- Why did the client make the request?

- What were the events that led to the request?

- How significant is the project to the client's organization?

- Is the client willing to provide staff resources to get the work done?

- Does the project have the support of management at a level consistent with the project's significance?

- What results does the client expect? In what time frame? At what general cost (range)?

- Does the client have some ideas about how the work ought to be done? What are they? How strongly are those ideas held?

- How many departments will be affected? Do these departments see the project benefiting them? Or threatening them?

Do you need to reassess the project?

- Based on what you know after the initial fact finding, should you change your decision to pursue the opportunity?

- Is the scope of the planned work realistic?

- Can the work be done cost-effectively?

How do you show the potential client the way you work?

- By the degree to which you've done your homework on the client's business:

  —What are the key processes? What are their products/services? What descriptive terms and unique vocabulary do they use?

- What are the client's goals? (You can identify some of these from recent trends in operations and financial management, and others from some of the responses you receive during fact-finding interviews.)

- What problems are common to the industry?

  In financial reporting?

  In management control?

  In operational planning?

- What problems are specific to the client's firm?

- By the way you ask questions:

  —Broad enough to allow a wide range of responses

  —Structured so that you spend your time listening, not talking

  —Using the client's frame of reference:

    - Industry and company language/terminology

    - Processes particular to the company

- By your professional demeanor that is conveyed by:

  —Your readiness to listen

  —Your concern for understanding the situation

  —The quality of your background information

  —The degree to which you are prepared to discuss the client's situation intelligently

  —The caliber and consistency of your people

- **First:**   You have to be prepared.

  Second: You have to demonstrate the way you work and think.

  Third: Most important—you have to come through at each moment of truth.

IDENTIFYING CONSULTING PROSPECTS

WHAT

Current Clients

Identify opportunities for extending services by being involved, knowing clients' needs, and being able to identify situations for additional services.

Referrals

Consultants can use this strategy as a relatively low-cost, low-risk way to enlarge the client base.

Community

Community visibility provides short-term as well as long-term results, although this technique is generally used for its benefits over the long term.

New Clients

Acquiring new clients is a necessity for a firm's healthy growth and an essential part of a consulting business. All the expertise and technical talents in the world are meaningless without clients.

WHY

Current Clients

Expansion of services to existing clients not only to increase revenue but also to have closer client relationships.

Referrals

There is negligible cost associated with this technique. The critical issue with referrals is the need for a systematic, disciplined approach to requesting them.

Community

As with other strategies, achieving community visibility is heavily dependent on the specific individuals who choose to be involved. The consultant who implements this strategy should be a good communicator and genuinely enjoy being involved in community activities and have time set aside for them.

New Clients

Acquisition of new business is often directly related to personal relationships with people in a position to refer business.

HOW

Current Clients

Personnel should be constantly alert to the possibilities of expanding services by bringing the expertise of all the departments to bear on clients problems.

Referrals

Success with this approach requires:

- Having a formal referral program in place

- Assigning specific responsibilities to individuals

- Maintaining a log of the requests

- Tracking the results of the program

Community

Volunteering one's services generally involves the commitment of time and some small expense. This is especially the case with such activities as service on the board of directors of charitable groups, involvement in fundraisers, and service on special committees and task forces. Consultants who attend and participate in these meetings find themselves in proximity to executives of prospective clients. Serving on committees keeps a firm visible and provides a sense of social contribution.

New Clients

When such a relationship exists and a need arises, the opportunity to make a presentation to a prospective client may be developed, and a new client may result. The development of these relationships is the responsibility of the rainmakers and other members of the firm aspiring to the rainmaker role.

WHEN

Current Clients

Personnel should be alert to opportunities for service and should become sufficiently knowledgeable about clients' affairs and current developments to recognize service opportunities.

Referrals

The strategy basically consists of asking a prior (and it's hoped satisfied) client to refer the consultant to other companies and prospective clients. Attorneys, bankers, and other noncompetitive consulting practitioners are also frequently asked to refer prospective clients.

Community

Community visibility programs focus on the long term. This can be considered a drawback to a firm seeking more immediate results. A number of new contacts will be initiated in the short term, but they may not produce dramatic short-term results.

New Clients

Many such relationships take years to cultivate. It is thus imperative that they begin at the earliest possible time in a professional career.

These relationships may be developed by active memberships in community, civic, and business organizations; through social contacts, client contacts, professional contacts, and reputation-building activities—for example, articles and speeches.

CLIENT PROFILE

CLIENT'S INDUSTRY TRENDS & DIRECTIONS

*Top Three Industry Trends
and Directions*   *Information Discovered*

- Major Industry Trend   _____

- Key Issues   _____

- Key Applications/   _____
  Technologies
                           _____

                           _____

                           _____

                           _____

                           _____

                           _____

                           _____

Top Three Industry Trends and Directions	**Information Discovered**
• Major Industry Trend	_____
• Key Issues	_____
• Key Applications/ Technologies	_____
	_____
	_____
	_____
	_____
	_____
	_____
	_____

• Major Industry Trend	_____
• Key Issues	_____
• Key Applications/ Technologies	_____
	_____
	_____
	_____
	_____
	_____
	_____
	_____
	_____

CLIENT'S BASIC INFORMATION

Basic Information	*Information Discovered*
• Full Company Name	_____
• Company Locations	_____
• Company Key Messages	_____
	_____
	_____
	_____
	_____

• Key Ratios (ROI, ROA, ROE)	_____
• Cash Position	_____
• Key Investments	_____
• Credit Rating	_____
• Key Expenditures	_____
	_____

• Chairman of Board	_____
• Chief Executive Officer	_____
• Chief Operations Officer	_____
• Chief Financial Officer	_____
• Chief Information Officer	_____
• Chief Knowledge Officer	_____

CLIENT'S BUSINESS PROFILE

Business Profile	*Information Discovered*
• Company Vision	_____
• Company Goals	_____
• Company Strategic Plans	_____
	_____
	_____
• Key Measures of Success	_____
• Short Term	_____
	_____
	_____
	_____
• Key Initiatives	_____
• Business	_____
	_____
	_____
	_____
	_____
Management Style	_____
Leadership Style	_____
Empowerment Style	_____
Adaptive to Change	_____

CLIENT'S PRODUCTS & SERVICES DESCRIPTION

Products & Services

- Key Products
- Key Services

Information Discovered

Products are: _____

_____

_____

Services are: _____

_____

_____

Key Product/Service
Information

—Target Market

—Life Cycle

—Price Range

—How Sold (Channels)

—Key Industries Sold

—Key Customers

—Key Geographies Sold

Product/Service Info:

_____

_____

_____

_____

_____

_____

_____

_____

_____

_____

CLIENT'S MARKET SHARE & COMPETITORS

Market Share & Competitors	Information Discovered
• Market Share Position (By Key Product Group)	_____ _____
• Key Issues (By Key Product Group)	_____ _____ _____ _____ _____ _____
• Key Competitors (By Product Group)	_____ _____
• Why Competitors Have Edge	_____
• Client's Competitive Strategy	_____ _____ _____ _____ _____
• Executives Responsible for Key Account Management	_____ _____ _____ _____ _____

CLIENT'S INFORMATION TECHNOLOGY PROFILE

IT Profile	*Information Discovered*
• IT Vendors	
• Key IT Applications	
• Major IT Expenditures	
• Key IT Projects	

CLIENT INTERVIEW CHECKLIST

AREAS OF FOCUS DURING CONSULTING INTERVIEWS

The information you need to have in conducting the engagement falls into these categories:

- *Client:* What clarifies and helps understand the client's situation? (This helps in developing the findings and conclusions.)

- *Issue:* What helps you decide if the issue is resolveable:

  —within a reasonable time?

  —cost-effectively?

  —with a reasonable chance of success, both technically and in terms of a satisfied client?

The interview questions should be open-ended but framed to help the client provide relevant answers. Too much information can be as bad as too little if you end up with more than you can analyze before the reporting deadline.

You want to establish rapport and build credibility in the interview. You must craft questions designed to do both.

Ways to establish rapport and build credibility:

- Use a series of questions about an issue to discuss it in greater detail, to convey your understanding of the client's business, and to show your concern by having given it some thought.

- Use statements as questions (What if _____ ?; Would _____ change things around here?). This conveys your ability in problem solving.

Thinking about the interview questions in this way will help keep the interview on course.

Decide which two or three areas of competence you most want to convey to the client. These should be related to the issues you identified in your initial research. Develop a discussion guide to help you focus on the most important client issues.

Possible strategies are:

- Examples of how you've addressed problems in the past

- A series of analytical questions

- "What if" questions

Your questions to convey information will be the backbone of your approach to the problem. By having the client address them directly, you will have the context for your findings and conclusions.

In presenting your interview questions, keep in mind that your desire is to develop the client's confidence in your understanding of the issues and ability to solve the problem.

INTERVIEW PROCESS

Make an Appointment

Whenever a lengthy interview (more than 30 minutes) is desired or when making a new contact, it is highly advisable to make an appointment. This serves two major purposes. First, it ensures that the interviewee is available and minimizes the possible waste of time. Second, advance notice enables the interviewee to prepare and collect any necessary information.

Be Prepared

The interviewer must take great care to be prepared. You must be perfectly clear as to what you wish to obtain from the interview and whether this is fact or opinion. Draw up a list of questions to ensure that no points are missed. This will also have the effect of minimizing the need to go back to the interviewee later to obtain supplementary information.

State the Reason for the Interview

Whether or not the interviewee has previously been acquainted with the purpose of the meeting, you will prevent any possible misunderstanding by stating briefly the purpose at the start of the interview.

Use Interviewee's Language

Most departments within any organization have their own specialized jargon. Failure to understand this special internal client language may cause you to miss some of the information you require or, worse still, to misinterpret it.

PREINTERVIEW CHECKLIST

	YES	NO	TO DO

For First Interviews:

1. Have you received background ___ ___   _____
   information, such as:
   • organization charts?
   • existing documentation?

2. Are there special directives or ___ ___   _____
   policy statements you know
   about that need to be reviewed?

3. Have you called to confirm ___ ___   _____
   the interview appointment
   and verified:
   • the interview length?
   • the interview location?
   • who will be interviewing?
   • the purpose of the interview?

4. Have you reviewed the ___ ___   _____
   interview strategy with
   your interview team
   member (if you have one)?

5. Interview strategy: ___ ___   _____
   • Who will ask questions?
   • Who will take notes?
   • Does one member of the team
     know the interviewee—how?
   • If so, does this affect your
     strategy?

6. Have you collected the ___ ___   _____
   material that you need for
   the interview, such as:
   • copies of the organization chart?
   • questions as a result of your
     background research?
   • probe questions?
   • documents?

POSTINTERVIEW CHECKLIST

	YES	NO	TO DO

1. Have you spent time with your ___ ___ _____
   interview team member to:
   * Discuss interview techniques that you both used?
     Were they successful? What didn't work? What would
     you both do differently? What would you do the same?
   * Discuss terms, phrases, and concepts
     that you didn't understand?

2. Did you schedule ___ ___ _____
   another interview?

3. Did you promise some ___ ___ _____
   follow-up tasks to the
   interviewee? Copies of your notes?

4. Have you documented the ___ ___ _____
   results of your interview, such as:
   * the organization?
   * the persons interviewed?
   * the tasks?
   * the data elements?
   * unresolved questions?
   * special notes?
   * key issues?

5. Are there other people who ___ ___ _____
   should be interviewed who were
   identified as a result of this interview?
   * Have you scheduled the
     interviews with these people?

6. Have you prepared a summary? ___ ___ _____
   * Have you highlighted the
     commonalties and particular uses
     of data, the tasks performed, etc.?

7. Are there still unresolved ___ ___ _____
   questions? Are there any uncompleted tasks
   that need to be done? Have you prepared
   additional specific questions, if necessary?

FOR FOLLOW-UP INTERVIEWS

	YES	NO	TO DO

1. Did you make an appointment ___ ___ _____
   for the follow-up interview
   during the first interview?

2. Have you called to reconfirm ___ ___ _____
   the date and time?
   • If you cannot attend the follow-up
     interview, have you told the person
     to be interviewed who will be
     conducting the interview?

3. Have you reviewed the ___ ___ _____
   postinterview documentation,
   such as:
   • tasks from the first interview?
   • the documents?
   • special notes from the session?
   • questions as a result of the session?

4. Are there unresolved ___ ___ _____
   questions as a result of the
   first interview? Have you
   prepared a list of questions
   to ask or points you want to
   clarify at this session?
   • What wasn't covered?
   • What wasn't clear to you?

5. Is there anything you ___ ___ _____
   promised that you need
   to follow up on?

6. If you are on an interview ___ ___ _____
   team, do the same strategy
   questions apply as in the
   first interview?

7. Have you collected the ___ ___ _____
   materials you need for
   the interview?

A

Accountability, 114, 181, 183–84
Advertising, 61
Advisors, Trusted, 10–12
Alignment, 135–36, 145
Audit partners, skills of, 5
Automobile sales, 6–7

B

Back-to-the-field programs, 37
Barcus, Sam, 11, 92–93, 160
Bartels, Jerry, 208
Baseball analogy, 116–18, 155–56
Batten, Joe D., 98–99
Bennett, Michael, 77
Bidding, 9, 10, 112, 183–91
    bidding case study, 186–89
    sales relationships and, 189
Brainstorming, 150, 153, 171, 176–80
Bryant, Kobe, 91
Business acumen, 53–54
Business partner, 33–34
Business process reengineering, 55

C

Canion, Rod, 158–59
Career development track, 29–30
Carnegie, Dale, 103
Chain of command, 24–25
Chambers, John, 48
Change control, 117–18
Cisco Systems, 7, 63, 157–58
    briefing model, 47–48

executive bonus payments,
    119–20
executive sponsorship program,
    48–49
Internet Business Solutions
    Group (ISBG), 17
voice over IP solutions, 16–17
Client
    vs. customer, 18–19
    expectations, 114
    profile. *See* Client profile
    relationships, partners and, 35
Client profile, 231–42
    basic information, 233
    business profile, 234
    industry trends/directions,
        231–32
    information technology profile,
        237
    interview checklists, 238–42
    market share/competitors, 236
    products/services description,
        235
Closed questions, 125–27
Collaboration, 91–93
Commissions, 61–62
Commoditization, 41, 58, 61, 64
Communication
    facilitation, 95–99
    feedback meetings and, 114–15
    presentation, 94–95
    style, 93–99
Community involvement, 33, 34,
    208
Company organization, 73
Compaq, 158–59

Compass. *See* Diagnostic Compass
Competency profiles, 217–24
    core competencies, 217–18
    engagement administration,
        219–20
    for partners, 222–23
    people development, 220–21
    personal characteristics, 221
    working characteristics, 218–19
Competitive issues, 55–57
Consulting cultures
    client/customer differences,
        18–19
    identifying prospects, 227–30
    independent orientation, 13–14
    knowledge of customers'
        executives, 12
    partner skills, 4, 5
    personal references, 15
    problem identification/solving,
        15–17, 19
    promise keeping, 17–18
    special training/qualifications,
        14–15
    and traditional businesses
        compared, 18–20, 22
    trust and, 10–12
Content questions, 128–30
Continuing education, 14
Corporate culture, 44, 73
Corporate politics, 74
Cott, Jonathan, 96–97
Creation cycle. *See* Wheel of Fortune
Credibility, 15, 88, 89–90, 92
Crossing the Chasm (Moore), 57
Customer data management, 203
Customer mind-share, 189
Customer relationship management
    (CRM), 3–4, 193–203, 216
    data application, 198
    executive relationship to data,
        199–200
    rainmakers and, 199–200
    technology *vs.* human touch,
        201–2
Customer retention, 206
Customers, reassignment of, 4
Customer Satisfaction Survey, 118–19

Customization, 19
Cycle Collision, 62–63

D

Delegation, 27–28
Dell, 7
Diagnosis
    diagnostic meetings, 91, 168–69
    engagement model and, 111–13
Diagnostic Compass, 143–63
    baseball analogy, 155–56
    conversational flow, 147–48
    80/20 rule, 150–51
    follow-up, 151
    going backward, 157–59
    interview dialogue, 146
    presentation, 155
    second meeting, 151–54
    solution phase, 149
Dialogue creation, 127
Dobson, James, 127

E

e-commerce solutions, 120
80/20 rule, 150–51
Elevator pitch, 95
Empathy, 107
Encore, 62–64
Engagement letter, 79, 113
Engagement model, 109–21
    diagnosis, 111–13
    illustrated, 110–11
    tactics *versus* strategy, 118–20
Engagements, 89
Enlightened Leadership (Oakley and
    Krug), 98
Evaluation criteria, 171
Executive briefings, 46–48
Executive meetings
    Diagnostic Compass and,
        143–50, 168
    80/20 rule, 150–51
    focus on client, 144–47
    follow-up, 151
    presentation, 155–56

sales reps and, 206–7
second meeting, 151–54
Executive sponsorship programs,
45–46, 48–49

F

Facilitation, 95–96
FBR: Feature-Benefit-Reaction, 8–9,
16, 185
Feedback meetings, 114–15
FFF: Feel-Felt-Found, 10, 16, 185
First-strike engagement, 23–25
Forecasts, 26
Friendships, 7
Fulfill phase, 61–62

G

Galbraith, John Kenneth, 96
GE Financial Services, 78
General Electric Corporation, 78
Georges, Jim, 105
Gerstner, Louis, 210–11
Glenn, John, 189–90
Goals, 55
Grove, Andy, 63
Gunslingers, 37

H–I

Hewlett-Packard, 7
*How to Win Friends and Influence
People* (Carnegie), 103
IBM, 7, 20–21, 36–37, 78, 115, 154,
157–58, 209–11
executive briefings, 46–47
Intensive Account Planning, 80
Oscar Mayer and, 80–83
Risc 6000 solutions, 16
Influence Model, 89–90
Initial Benefit Statement (IBS), 9
Initial research, 72–73
Innovators, 57–62, 191
Installation, 118
Intel Corporation, 63
Interest, expressing, 104–8, 115, 216

Internet
communication and, 3
solutions, 120
Internet Business Solutions Group
(IBSG), 17
Interrogative leadership style, 99
Interview checklists, 238–42
follow-up interviews, 242
postinterview checklist, 241
preinterview checklist, 240
Interviews, 73, 215
communication style and, 96–99
participation, 98–99
questions. *See* Questions

K–L

King, Larry, 96
Krug, Doug, 98
Laggards, 57–58
Letter of understanding, 79
Listening skills, 98–99
Loyalty Effect, The (Reichheld), 205–6
Loyalty Rules! (Reichheld), 205–6

M

Machado, Antonio, 96–97
Manage phase, 61, 64
Managers, 31–32
managing director, 33
style of, and problem solving,
175
Manipulation, 8
Marketing Life Cycle, 59–60
Mentoring, 30, 31, 37, 99–100, 152,
154, 215
partners and, 34
rainmakers and, 69
Mission, 55
Moore, Geoffrey, 57–60, 60

N–O

Negotiation, 100
New product introductions, 60
Oakley, Ed, 98
Objectives, 55, 75

Objectivity, 13–14
Obstacles
    defining, 176–77
    prioritizing, 177–79
O'Neal, Shaquille, 91
Open questions, 127–35
    see also Questions
    content questions, 128–30
    process questions, 130–34, 162
Operational issues, 55
Opportunity Assessment Matrix,
    75–77, 215
Organization chart, 24
Oscar Mayer, Inc., 80–83
Outcome statement, 169–72
Outplacement, 31, 37

P

Packaging, 56
PAR Group, 104, 105, 135–36
Partners, 33–35
    career path of, 36
    client relationships and, 35
    community involvement and, 34
    competency profiles for, 222–23
    as rainmakers, 35
Partnership pyramid. See Peer-level
    matchups; Pyramid
Peer-level matchups, 39–51, 206–11,
    212–13
    see also Pyramid
    case study, 40–44
    Cisco Systems and, 47–49
    practical approaches, 45–49
    traditional businesses and,
        44–45
Performance management, 114
Personal behaviors/traits/feelings, 7
Planning issues, 55–57
Politics (corporate), 74
Pop quizzes, 24, 35, 180
Practice development, 101
Practice leaders, 32
Practices, 32
Presentation, 155–56
Price/pricing
    bidding. See Bidding

focus, 55
in partnership, 64–66
PricewaterhouseCoopers, 29, 32–33,
    210
    Enterprise Resource Planning,
        78
Problem identification/solving,
    15–17, 99–100, 167–82
    business processes/procedures
        and, 175
    constructing desired outcome,
        169–72
    defining the obstacles, 176–77
    diagnostic team meeting,
        168–69
    management style and, 175
    people issues, 175
    policies impacting, 175
    problem situation statement,
        172–76
    problem-solving template,
        169–70, 173
    qualifiers, 173–76
    rainmakers and, 99–100, 180–81
    solution, 177–80
Process methodology, 34
Process questions, 130–34
Product
    delivery, 118
    introductions, 60
    life cycles, 57–62
Project management, 32
Promise keeping, 17–18
Promise of satisfaction, 18
Proposals, developing/presenting,
    78–80
Prospects, 71–72
    initial research of, 72–73
    interviewing, 73
    qualifying, 74–75, 215
Public relations, 61
Purchasing departments, 56, 208
Purchasing managers, 61
Pyramid, 27–35, 39–40, 207–8
    see also Peer-level matchups
    first-strike engagement, 23–25
    managers, 31–32
    missing link, 26–27

partners, 33–35
rainmakers and, 27–35
sales quotas *versus* strategy, 25–26
senior managers, 32–33
senior staff, 30–31
staff, 29–30
structure, 152
and traditional business
 practices compared, 35

Q

Qualitative issues, 174–76
Quantitative issues, 173–74
Questions, 123–39
 alignment and, 135–36
 closed/quid pro quo, 125–27
 dialogue creation and, 127
 during diagnostic meetings, 170
 interviews and, 98
 nonalignment and, 137–38
 open, 127–35
 wrong types of, 124–25
Quid pro quo questions, 125–27
Quota, 60

R

Rainmakers, 28, 35
 accountability of, 114, 181,
  183–84
 client engagements and. *See*
  Wheel of Fortune
 mentoring and, 69, 99–100
 negotiation and, 100
 practice development and, 101
 as problem solvers, 99–100,
  180–81
 process and, 69
 relationship development. *See*
  Engagement model
 strategy development and, 65
 team building and, 100
Raising Boys (Dobson), 127
Referrals, 87
Reichheld, Frederick, 205–6
Relationships, 3, 88–93
 collaboration, 91–93

evolution of trusted, 89–91
relationship advantage, 4
trust and, 6–8
Reputation, 88
Research, 72–73, 215
Resetting the mood, 127, 132, 143,
 144, 160
Resources, 76–77
Rhetorical questions, 124
Risk, sharing, 117
Rolling Stone, 96
Rosen, Ben, 158–59

S

Sales/selling
 and bidding compared, 183–91
 commissions, 61–62
 defining needs prior to, 184
 quotas *versus* strategy, 25–26
 reassignment of territories, 4
 sales calls, and interviews
  compared, 73
 sales engagement process,
  118–19
 sales quotas *versus* strategy,
  25–26
 sales reps, 206–8
 training. *See* Sales training
 trust and, 6–7
Sales training, 3, 4, 7–10, 37–38
 FBR: Feature-Benefit-Reaction,
  8–9
 FFF: Feel-Felt-Found, 10
 IBS: Initial Benefit Statement, 9
Schaffer, Bill, 81–82, 106
Senior management, 32–33
Senior staff, 30–31
Services, life cycles and, 59
Shipping, 60–61
Shopworn questions, 125
Social involvement opportunities,
 208
Solution
 phase, 149
 presentation, 155–57
 providers, 16
Specialization areas, 32

Staff, 29–30
Strategic issues, 54–55
Strategy development, 65
Success, ensuring, 88–89
    communication style, 93–99
    relationships, 88–93
    reputation, 88
Sun Microsystems Sparc server
    solutions, 16
Supply and demand, 7

T

Tactical issues, 55
Team building, 100
Team meetings (problem solving),
    168–69
Technology Adoption Life Cycle,
    The, 57–62
Terkel, Studs, 96–97
Time-Place-Price benefit, 187
Tough-Minded Leadership (Batten), 98
Trick questions, 124
Trust, 5–8, 88–89, 90–91, 92
    interpersonal actions and, 106
    respect and, 129

Trusted Advisors, 10–12

V

Value, 58
    in partnership, 64–66
    and price focus, 55
Value-added resellers (VARs), 187–88
Value Staircase, 54–57, 184–85, 191,
    207
Vendor status, 157–59
Vision, 55

W–Y

Wheel of Fortune, 69–83, 101
    creation cycle tactics, 224–26
    develop/present proposal, book
        engagement, 78–80
    initial research, 72–73
    interview, 73
    Oscar Mayer and, 80–83
    prospects, 71–72
    qualify, 74–78, 215
Yamaha Band Instrument Company,
    77